Stepping Out on Faith

STEPPING OUT ON FAITH

Jerry Falwell
and Elmer Towns

Tyndale House
Publishers, Inc.
Wheaton, Illinois

All Scripture references are taken from the
King James Version unless otherwise indicated.

First printing, October 1984
Library of Congress Catalog Card Number 84-50975
ISBN 0-8423-6626-1

CONTENTS

INTRODUCTION   9

1 FAITH TO MOVE MOUNTAINS
by Jerry Falwell   15

2 LIGHTHOUSE BAPTIST CHURCH
Alfred Henson, Pastor   29

3 HERITAGE BAPTIST CHURCH
Rod Kidd, Pastor   39

4 HOLY MOUNTAIN
BAPTIST CHURCH
Steve Ray, Pastor   47

5 WACHUSETT VALLEY
BAPTIST CHURCH
John Martelli, Pastor   57

6 HARVEST BAPTIST CHURCH
Marvin Wood, Pastor   67

7 CALVARY ROAD
BAPTIST CHURCH
David Rhodenhizer, Pastor   77

8 FREEPORT BAPTIST CHURCH
Kurt Strong, Pastor   89

9 NEW LIFE BAPTIST CHURCH
Ronnie Riggins, Pastor 97

10 FREDERICKTOWNE
BAPTIST CHURCH
Gary Byers, Pastor 105

11 BALTIMORE COUNTY
BAPTIST CHURCH
Bob Gehman, Pastor 115

12 SPIRITUAL GIFTS
AND CHURCH GROWTH 123

13 ANSWERING QUESTIONS
ABOUT SPIRITUAL GIFTS 129

14 THE GIFT
OF FAITH 145

15 HOW TO APPLY
THE GIFT OF FAITH 165

APPENDIX I
Measuring Ten Attitudes of Faith 177

APPENDIX II
*Statistics of the Ten Liberty
Churches with the Fastest DGR* 202

APPENDIX III
Questionnaire 205

APPENDIX IV
Interview Questions 207

ENDNOTES 209

BIBLIOGRAPHY 217

FOREWORD
by C. Peter Wagner

Elmer Towns and Jerry Falwell have written several books on church growth, and I have read most of them. This work stands with the best. They deal with the theme of faith and its specific relationship to church growth, demonstrating convincingly that faith is the key to building a church. Thus, this book on church growth breaks new ground. Church growth is more than a science based on sociological principles; it is based on the power of God.

Their research model is excellent. Narrowing the field to churches started by the new Liberty Baptist Fellowship movement gives a basis for drawing insight into the church growth principles that work. Since most of the Liberty churches share a similar philosophy of ministry, the variables become more prominent. Also, the measurement of faith taken among the pastors of the fastest growing churches was very appropriately compared to the measured faith level of Liberty Baptist pastors in general. Developing and testing the instrument to measure faith is an obvious advance in church growth research and thinking.

I like the taxonomy of faith as instrumental, insightful, and interventional. The self-perception of the pastors who were interviewed for the case studies demonstrated the validity of the classification. I think this book will be used widely to motivate other books on faith and church growth in various denominations as they do the same study.

The case studies of the ten churches are thrilling. Some of the tremendous blessings of God actually brought tears to my eyes. I was fascinated, for example, that Rod Kidd started a church in Lynchburg, right in the shadow of Thomas Road. And it is a healthy, growing church.

Chapters 12 through 14 provide a well-documented and carefully reasoned study of the concept of the gift of faith. I know of no other literature which handles this matter so extensively. I believe this will become a reference point for others who deal with any aspect of the field of spiritual gifts.

This was an enjoyable work to read and is one of the best church growth books written recently. I will use it as required reading in my class on planting new churches. Elmer Towns' part of the book was his D. Min. dissertation at Fuller Theological Seminary, where it received a commendation for excellence. Jerry Falwell's part of the book was his tremendous leverage and expression of faith that motivated the ten men who built the ten churches.

C. Peter Wagner

INTRODUCTION

It has been said that a person could pry the earth from its orbit with a lever long enough and a fulcrum strong enough. For through the dynamics of leverage, a person can vastly intensify his energy. But there must be a solid foundation on which to base the lever.

Faith is the most powerful lever available to man, because with it he can move the mightiest force in the universe—Almighty God. But the leverage of faith must be grounded on the eternal Word of God. Just as a lever is powerless without a solid point from which to extend its power, so faith is ineffective when it is disassociated from God's revelation of himself and his will.

This book examines how men have used faith in the work of God. They have raised millions of dollars, built buildings, overcome speech impediments, and accomplished victories. They have captured their towns and planted churches by faith.

The faith of these men appears to be greater or different than the faith of the average person. Therefore an examination was made to determine what it was that made their faith so effective. It was found that they possessed the biblical quality called "the gift of faith," which is one of the serving gifts that God has made available to the church. This book attempts to examine and measure the gift of faith.

The motivation for this book grew out of a historic conviction that the faith of the pastor was one of the main reasons for the growth of large churches.[1] When Elmer Towns became involved with Jerry Falwell, Pastor of the Thomas Road Baptist Church in Lynchburg, Virginia, he felt that faith was the greatest spiritual gift possessed by Falwell. Faith was also the source of growth for the church.[2] However, Towns did nothing with this conviction until Peter Wagner suggested to him that the spiritual gifts of faith and leadership were the common denominator that he found in the pastors of the largest churches. Wagner went on to explain that the pastors he observed in large churches had different gifts that were responsible for the growth of their churches; some pastors produced growth through preaching while others were only average speakers. Some pastors produced growth through administration, counseling, or teaching; but Wagner felt that all the pastors of large churches had the spiritual gift of faith. Wagner writes, "The super church pastors I know all have this gift [the gift of faith]. . . . I had come to the conclusion that God had given him [a pastor] the gift of faith."[3]

Almost no research or comprehensive discussion was found on the spiritual gift of faith. The topic is usually discussed briefly in the material dealing with spiritual gifts, but usually the material on the spiritual gift of faith is covered in a paragraph or at the most a few pages. Whole books and dissertations are given over to the discussion of spiritual gifts, while the topic of faith in church growth has been neglected too long. The authors contend that the spiritual gift of faith is one of the foundational abilities for church growth or any work for God; and those who have accomplished much for God have exercised the spiritual gift of faith.

In chapter 1 Falwell relates the gift of faith in church planting and church growth to four areas. First, faith was related to choosing a location; second, faith was related to the message upon which the churches were built (doctrine); third, faith was related to carrying out the objectives of the church; and, fourth, faith was related to applying the principles of church growth learned at Liberty.

A survey was sent to the churches pastored by Liberty (seminary, college, and institute) graduates who were influenced by Falwell to examine their faith in these four areas. The authors used Decadal Growth Rate to determine the ten fastest growing churches among the Liberty graduates. The growth of these churches is included in chapters 2-11. Only those Liberty churches which had been in existence for five years and had built or purchased a permanent location were included in this book. It was felt that a new church could attract large crowds but had not significantly influenced its "Jerusalem" until it could purchase land and construct a building.

In chapter 12, the phrase *spiritual gift* is examined in both the New Testament and contemporary literature with a view of arriving at a workable understanding of the abilities that a Christian possesses for serving the Lord. In chapter 14 the three definitions given of the gift of faith in literature are examined: (1) instrumental, (2) insightful, and (3) interventional. These three aspects of faith are examined both theologically and practically in light of their use in serving the Lord. Even though there seem to be three different ways that the gift of faith is interpreted in literature, the authors believe that these three aspects are three cumulative steps in exercising the gift of faith.

This research was carried out by Towns as a doctoral dissertation at Fuller Theological Seminary, Pasadena, California. It involved a narrow church group, Liberty graduates, because of the general reputation they enjoy regarding the relationship of their faith to church growth. But the findings from a controlled group are more likely to reveal a pattern; hence, conclusions might be easily observed which would give insight to the hypothesis that the gift of faith as perceived and applied by the church leaders is one of the factors for their success in church growth.

However, even with the controlled group (same higher educational institution, same human motivation such as Jerry Falwell, and same support system such as Liberty Baptist Fellowship), the ten pastors differ in the nature of their faith and the expression of faith. Many might have expected all Liberty men to be in close agreement because of the explicit expectations of "faith and polity" by the Liberty Baptist Fellowship. But their differences are that they are human, the Holy Spirit leads differently, and their community context differs. But with their differences there is general agreement; explained by Paul: "Now there are diversities of gifts, but the same Spirit. And there are differences of ministries, but the same Lord. And there are diversities of activities, but it is the same God who works all in all" (1 Cor. 12:4–6, NKJV).

When we speak of the gift of faith, we may be referring to one of three interpretations of the phrase. These are explained in some detail in chapter 14, but since we refer to them throughout the book, perhaps a brief explanation at this point might be helpful.

Some say the gift of faith is an *instrument*, something to be used in Christian services as one would use the Bible, the gift of administration, the gift of preaching. This is the *instrumental* view, which appears to be the way most people speak of it.

Others think of the gift of faith as the ability to see or perceive what God desires to accomplish. This is called the *insight* or *vision* view. With this gift one could see what God wants to accomplish and then uses every resource available to bring it to pass.

The third view is that the gift of faith is the ability to move God to divinely intervene to accomplish his work. This is the *interventional* view. To those who hold this view, the day of miracles is not passed, but such miracles are still available to us today—especially to those who can, with the gift of faith, claim them for ministering the gospel.

May this volume have a twofold contribution to Christianity. First, may it stimulate the faith of many to trust God for greater things. Second, may it motivate others to plant New Testament churches to the glory of God.

Jerry Falwell
Elmer Towns
Liberty Mountain
Lynchburg, Virginia

1
FAITH TO MOVE MOUNTAINS
by Jerry Falwell

I accepted Christ as my Savior in January 1952. The Bible describes this as: "For by grace are ye saved through faith" (Eph. 2:8). To me, faith was simply putting my trust in Jesus Christ to save me from sin. My faith became effective by its object, Jesus Christ. That initial act of faith molded my whole perspective of living for Christ and serving Christ. I learned that I not only had to be saved by faith, but live by faith and serve by faith.

The foundation of my faith is the Word of God, which is called *the faith* in Scripture. When the word *faith* is technically identified by the article *the,* it is a reference to doctrine or to the statement of faith. A person's faith is not measured by his internal trust but by the objective truth of the Word of God.

I have never doubted the existence of God, nor did I question the creation of the universe by God in six literal days. When I was saved, I accepted the literal inspiration and accuracy of every word of Scripture. There has never been a question in my mind concerning the virgin birth, the substitutionary death of Christ for sin, his physical resurrection from the dead, or his bodily return. These are the doctrinal foundations of Christianity that are called our statement of faith. My personal faith for salvation, my daily walk with God, and my faith to serve God are all built upon the unquestionable certainty of doctrinal faith.

When I went to Baptist Bible College in Springfield, Missouri, I encountered people who were trusting God for every aspect of their lives. They were living by faith, and I wanted to have the same type of walk with God. These people were trusting God to take care of their financial needs. My parents were not wealthy, but they were comfortable. I had been given $4,000 before I went off to school. I knew the promises in Scripture that God would take care of me. I wanted to put God to the test when he said, "prove me now" (Mal. 3:10). As an act of faith, I gave away the $4,000 to needy individuals, the school, and the church.

During these early formative days of my Christian life, I asked the dean of students for a key to an empty dormitory room. Each afternoon after lunch, I went there and began praying for God's blessing on my life. I read books by such great men as R. A. Torrey, Hudson Taylor, Watchman Nee, and others who lived by faith. These books, plus the messages I heard at college, challenged me to trust God for everything.

I had a new Buick that my mother had given me. I needed gas to use it in Sunday school visitation, so May Hawkins provided me a Texaco account so I could fill it up whenever necessary. God used others to meet my needs. It seemed every time a godly Christian businessman passed me at church, he put a twenty-dollar bill in my hand.

I believe God was motivating these men and others to provide for my needs. They gave to me, not just because I was needy or was one of the Baptist Bible College students. I believe they gave to me, and not to other students just as needy as I, because they knew I was actively serving the Lord and needed money to win souls to Jesus Christ. I had taken a Sunday school class at High Street Baptist Church with only one pupil and built the class to over fifty students in one year. God honors the faith of those who are actively using their lives to serve him.

The secret of trusting God for $10 million is found in trusting God for $10. Just as I needed one dollar for a tank of gas to go soul-winning, today I need $10 million to preach the gospel on television and build a college to train church planters. I can honestly say I have never asked for money for my personal needs. God has always provided for me. But I am not hesitant to ask for money for the work of God.

When I returned to Lynchburg to begin the Thomas Road Baptist Church, I became aggressive in trying to win souls and reaching the city for Jesus Christ. I was going door to door, trying to win people to Christ. To reach the entire city by the most efficient means possible, I immediately began a daily radio program. When I realized that people were watching TV, I prayed that God would open the door to television. When the opportunity came, I knew God would supply the finances because we were carrying out the Great Commission.

Perhaps some have tried to raise money for a radio or television ministry and failed, not because God did not hear their prayers, but perhaps because their motives were not singularly dedicated to carrying out the purpose of God to win souls and edify Christians. I do not think the gift of faith is given to someone to raise money or solve problems, apart from his aggressively fulfilling the Great Commission that God has given to the church. When faith is removed from the commands of Scripture, it no longer is biblical faith.

When we faced our first anniversary at Thomas Road Baptist Church, we wanted to demonstrate the power of God to Lynchburg. Every Sunday before the evening service I met with several men, including Emmitt Godsey (who still leads this prayer meeting), to pray for God's blessing. We met in a small room with a dirt floor. It was there that God burdened us to set a goal of 500 people for our first anniversary.

I realize that some critics have misunderstood why we set goals; but I believe faith moves mountains and glorifies God. Faith is not only an instrument; it enables us to intervene in problems and overcome obstacles. The church had 864 on its first anniversary. That victory reinforced my faith to trust God for bigger goals. Paul challenges us to go "from faith to faith" (Rom. 1:17), which I interpret to mean going from one victory by faith to another.

It seems we have always been setting goals and making them. A memorable goal was to have 10,000 in attendance for Harvest Day, 1971. The ministers met at a local restaurant and discussed what our goal should be. At the time, our attendance averaged just over 4,000 each week. We had already had 5,000. Dr. Towns told us that someday our Sunday school would have 10,000. I thought we ought to demonstrate that God could glorify himself in a small, central Virginia town by doing what everyone thought was impossible.

Jesus had promised, "If ye have faith as a grain of mustard seed, ye shall say unto this mountain, Remove hence to yonder place; and it shall remove; and nothing shall be impossible unto you" (Matt. 17:20). Based on the Word of God, I knew we could reach 10,000. I knew that if soul-winning was our aim, God would have to bless us. But I also knew faith and works go hand in hand (James 2). We organized and worked, saturating Lynchburg by every conceivable means. We had 10,187 in attendance with 157 decisions at the altar.

Starting the college was a step of faith in every way—

trusting God for teachers, money, facilities, and students. I prayed about a goal and felt God would give us 100 students. Later, Dr. Towns told me that he felt I had set the goal too high. He had been a college president and knew how hard it was to recruit students. He thought 50 was even high. I had no human experience on which to set the goal; I just said what God put on my heart. Without Dr. Towns' experience in recruitment, we could not have done it. Even God's sending him to be the co-founder of Liberty was the result of faith. It was a step of faith for both of us, and we began the college with 153 students on September 8, 1971.

Quite often I get letters from people questioning why we have so many financial crises at Liberty or the Old Time Gospel Hour. I do not feel we should let up or turn back. We have the command of God to go into all the world and win people to Christ. With that staggering command we have the promise that God will supply our every need. I believe God can be trusted to help us to do what he has commanded.

As I write this chapter, I have challenged our people to pray for $10 million (June 1983). We have continued to build new buildings on Liberty Mountain for the college, and we have continued to broadcast the gospel on over 500 radio and 300 television stations. Since we have done what God has commanded, I expect God to provide $10 million to take care of the bills.

A newspaper reporter asked me, "Suppose the money does not come in; what will happen?"

"We do not think that way," I told her.

"Just suppose," the reporter again asked.

"I am not even willing to do that," I replied.

Since God has promised to meet our needs, why should I doubt his integrity by even considering less than his promise?

I have never tried to give a complete systematic explanation of faith to the ministry students at Liberty. I believe in what has been called the "hot poker" method of communicating faith. Just as the poker is heated in the fire, I believe these young ministers learn to have faith in God as they trust God with us for the buildings in which they study and the sidewalks on which they walk. They learn faith by exercising faith.

I tell the young ministers at Liberty to "go and do it better and do it bigger." If a ministerial candidate accepts this challenge, his faith is stretched. He realizes he cannot begin a church by human means because it is not easy to plant a church. When a young man commits himself to plant a church, it is a "step of faith" in which he must overcome obstacles. With this challenge, the young man realizes he must grow in faith, overcoming the weakness of his faith. If these men accept the challenge to build a church (desire), they also realize their weak faith (reality); hence, they are placed in a crisis in which they must trust the power of God (interventional faith). As they exercise the first step of faith, if they are successful, they will grow in their ability to trust God for bigger projects.

There are four areas in which I challenge ministerial candidates to trust God in church planting: (1) trusting God to lead to the correct location; (2) trusting God to use the message in people's lives (doctrine); (3) trusting God to bless the unique objectives in planting a church; and (4) trusting God to bless specific principles to build a church. (These four areas are explained in Appendix I.)

A. *Faith and location.* The exercise of faith in church planting involves the identification of a city by the church planter, then acting on faith to go to that city and begin a church. I encourage them to: (1) pray over a location or city; (2) visit it to determine its social and religious conditions; (3) research the area so they are informed of its special needs and prospects; and (4) if the conditions are right and God has given a spiritual burden or leading to the city, announce their goals publicly. This expression of faith first takes reality when a church planter gives his future church a name before he goes to the location. Then he usually distributes prayer cards, announcing the church's name and location to help raise financial support.

He may request financial support by presenting an application to Liberty Baptist Fellowship. In order to have his request approved, the student must be specific in plans and purpose. LBF does not guarantee all his financial support. We provide him $150 per week in support, knowing that is not enough to support a family. He must go to his friends, relatives, and other churches to raise an additional $50 a week. (Most raise more support than this.) I feel that if a young man can trust God by successfully raising money for his church, he has learned one of the most integral parts of planting and building a church. Raising money is not the only criterion for church planting, but those who cannot raise money probably cannot plant a church.

Every step the church planter takes—from the initial burden and vision of the church (insightful faith) to winning souls through preaching the Word (instrumental faith)—until he arrives on location and overcomes obstacles (interventional faith), is part of the life of faith, described as "one faith" (Eph. 4:5).

B. *Faith and doctrine.* I challenge the young minister to be loyal to the fundamentals of the faith. Correct doctrine is the biblical foundation for evangelizing a community and building up believers into spiritual maturity.[1] The ministerial candidate must realize that his potential for success is tied to doctrinal faith.

The church planter must have complete faith in the content of his doctrine, believing that the gospel alone will build a church. When the church planter adds anything to the foundation of the church, it will fail.

By faith he trusts God to capture the hearts of people who will give their loyalty to Christ and express their devotion through the church he will build. By faith, he refuses to put his trust in his personality, financial support, or organizational ability. At Liberty, we teach the young men that the fundamentals of the faith are unquestionable. These are the irreducible, minimum doctrines of faith.

When a church planter doubts these doctrines, I fear he cannot build a New Testament church. I realize some liberals have begun organizations they call churches. When they deny the fundamentals of the faith they cannot have the blessing of God. They may build an organization and call it a church, just as a man may begin a business; but the work they have begun is not a New Testament church. There is no such thing as faith that is not grounded in the truth of God as found in Scripture.

C. *Faith and objectives.* I teach the ministerial candidates that the Great Commission is the objective of the church (Matt. 28:19, 20).[2] This was the mandate I followed in building Thomas Road Baptist Church; and if these young men will obey the same command, God will bless them. The Great Commission is a command to: (1) make disciples or win souls; (2) baptize converts and identify them with a local church; and (3) teach Christians so they can be built up to spiritual maturity. A young minister does not exercise faith by some esoteric expression of belief. When he tries to win as many lost people to Christ as he can, that is obedience to the Word of God—which is faith.

The next step of faith is not just to "fellowship" with new believers. The church planter must attempt to get them baptized into a local church; that is obedience to the Word of God—which is faith. Then the young minister must gather the converts together and teach them Scripture. When he is obeying these three commands, he is exercising faith. After he has obeyed the command of God, he can expect God to supply money to construct buildings so the work continues.

Some ministers have failed because they ostensibly trust God for money; but it does not come in, because the minister is not obeying the commands of Scripture and aggressively winning souls to Jesus Christ. I tell the young men that the church is God's organization for evangelism and that a pastor has the highest calling of God. The more carefully a minister carries out the Great Commission, the more God will bless both him and the new church.

I exhort the young men that a church is not a renewal group, nor is it one program among many that people may or may not join. The local church is God's priority at home and on the mission field. Those who plant churches are closest to the heart and plan of God; therefore, the church planter can exercise faith and expect the blessing of God on his ministry.

I make a correlation between success in church planting and carrying out the explicit objectives of the Great Commission. When a young man exercises faith in God by applying the exact steps of the Great Commission (1. winning souls; 2. baptizing them into a church; and 3. teaching them the Bible), he is fulfilling what he has been taught: i.e., that the new church will prosper. Some might argue that other churches have prospered without applying these explicit steps, but that is not the point. Liberty men express their faith in God by their obedience to what they perceive as literal objectives for church growth.[3]

D. *Faith and principles.* I challenge church planters to apply the principles of saturation evangelism to build a church. By this I mean, "Preach the gospel by every available means to every available person at every available time."[4] The young minister should take as his example the Jerusalem church and the

Antioch church to illustrate the success of the application of these principles.

The term *saturation evangelism* applies to the principle of completely covering a town with the gospel, just as a man uses a lawn sprinkler to saturate the ground so the grass will grow. If a young man will saturate his Jerusalem with the gospel by using visitation, posters, mailings, radio, television, billboards, etc., he will successfully build a church. He does not express faith by just praying for lost people to get saved; rather, faith is expressed by first praying, then aggressively going to as many people as possible and presenting the gospel to them. Faith is not passively waiting for people to come to your church; faith is actively going to the lost.

The term *super-aggressive evangelism* is another way of saying saturation evangelism. The phrase *super-aggressive* means to use all our energy and creative ability to get the gospel to people in a positive way so they will be saved. Super-aggressive refers to the enthusiasm and zeal with which the task is done. The key to understanding super-aggressive evangelism is to possess or be possessed by a vision of what God can do. The following verse explains the basis of saturation evangelism: "Ye have filled Jerusalem with your doctrine" (Acts 5:28). The purpose of a church is to fill its "Jerusalem" with the doctrine of Christ. When our Jerusalem, Lynchburg, is saturated, a person under conviction will think first of Thomas Road when he is searching for God. God is able to use saturation evangelism to lead sinners to a church where they can hear the gospel.

"And they continued stedfastly in the apostles' doctrine and fellowship, and in breaking of bread, and in prayers" (Acts 2:42). This is a description of phenomenal church growth. Three thousand had just been saved and baptized in one day. The Christians "continued stedfastly" in the work of God.

1. Christians made contact with every person in Jerusalem. Contact is essential.
2. Christians were continuous in their ministry. They were accused of having filled Jerusalem with their doctrine (Acts 5:28).
3. Christians had a consciousness of an unlimited ministry. There were no mental limitations to their ministry.

The Christians in Jerusalem realized that, although only a few thousand people were in their church, they had the responsibility of reaching the world. They also realized their outreach was as extensive as their faith and vision.

The program of the church is contact, continuous contact, with a consciousness of no limitations.

I tell some church planters that they may be in an area where the field is perhaps limited to 5,000 or 10,000 people in the immediate vicinity; that should not be reason for thinking they will soon saturate their city and be out of prospects. I found in Lynchburg, Virginia, a city of 72,000 people, that there is no limitation on what can be done. When our church started twenty-five years ago with a handful of people, we thought that reaching 500 would make a large church of saved people regularly serving the Lord. When we reached 500, we found ourselves going for 1,000. When we reached 1,000, we then prayed for 2,000, next 3,000, and finally 4,000. Now we average over 10,000 per Sunday.

The church at Jerusalem was accused of having filled Jerusalem with their doctrine (Acts 5:28). That simply means they had personally talked to every individual in Jerusalem and presented him with the claims of the gospel. Several years later they were accused of having turned the world upside down. They did all of this without television, radio, a printing press, automobiles, airplanes, or telephones. Today, saturation evangelism is filling one's "Jerusalem" with the gospel.

As Liberty students become involved in Christian service in Thomas Road Baptist Church, they "catch the spirit" of church growth. Usually, they see a weekly application of growth as they serve God in the church. After graduation, most students are convinced that the principles they were taught at one of the Liberty schools will produce growth in their new church.

Others have expressed their faith in God by applying church growth principles different from those taught at Liberty. Church growth has occurred in the work of Liberty students and of others. I realize it is faith that has produced church growth. The church planter must find principles that work for him and apply the principles by faith. We cannot speak for the others, but our Liberty men grow churches when they apply the saturation principles of the Word of God. Because saturation evangelism requires extensive outreach into the entire area, the student must have extensive faith.

CONCLUSION

I do not believe we give church planters their faith; we simply provide the challenge and opportunity to grow their faith. Faith comes from the Word of God (Rom. 10:17) and it grows as a young man actively applies the principles of Scripture to his life and ministry.

God seems to be restating the challenge of church planting to us; that is why we have set a goal of planting 5,000 new churches. I believe the eighties offer a unique challenge and opportunity to reach our nation for Christ. It seems as if God is giving us another chance to turn our country around. Why is this a unique time for church planting? Because time is limited; Christ is coming soon. By faith we accept that fact, and we must plant 5,000 new churches to reach as many lost people with the gospel as we can before it is too late.

Also, today we have vast technological aids to preaching the gospel. I preach to more people on one Sunday because of television than Wesley or Luther reached in a lifetime. By faith, a church planter must use every available means to reach every available person at every available time. Then, the social setting in our country demands church planting. Many conservative pastors are not aggressive soul-winners. No one is aggressively planting new churches, and the only way to reach this country is by new churches being started in the areas where the people are. The new suburbs constitute a legitimate need for new churches; we must begin new churches there. The mainline churches located in metropolitan areas should have held the line, but have abdicated their responsibilities. We must plant new churches or revitalize old ones in the metropolitan areas. No matter where new churches are located, the pastor must aggressively preach the gospel and saturate his "Jerusalem" with the gospel. It will take faith for him to see what can be accomplished (insightful faith); then he will need faith to apply the Word of God (instrumental faith); and finally, by faith he can overcome barriers that stand in the way of the work of God (interventional faith).

We must go into all the world and preach the gospel to every person. When we attempt to carry out this command, it is an act of faith that God will bless.

2
LIGHTHOUSE BAPTIST CHURCH
Nashville, Tennessee
Alfred Henson, Pastor

The largest and fastest-growing church planted by a Liberty graduate is also considered the strongest in many other ways. Al Henson left Liberty Baptist Seminary in 1978 and immediately began Lighthouse Baptist Church in the recreation room of an apartment complex. Because he believes faith intervenes in the problems that face the work of God, he fasted and prayed for twenty-five acres of ground on I-24. The provision of the ground was miraculous.

The church has constructed four buildings for a total worth of $2 million in assets, received an annual income of $963,000 in 1982, and has 425 students in a Christian school, plus the Institute of Discipleship (night institute with 95 enrolled). The church averages almost one thousand in attendance, has helped plant fifteen new churches in five states, and now has more than fifty Liberty graduates working for the church, or as evangelists and/or church planters. By numerical considerations, plus evidence of the same view of faith, Lighthouse reflects the impetus of Thomas Road Baptist Church and the outreach of Jerry Falwell.

Henson said that his first step of faith was selling everything and moving to Lynchburg, Virginia, to enroll in Liberty Baptist Seminary. "God was beginning to teach me daily faith." When his wife, Susan, applied for a job, the employer read someone else's application by mistake and gave the job to Susan. Henson sees this as the provision of God.

When Henson was a student at Liberty, he wanted to put God to the test. "I wanted to see a miracle so I would know that God's provision would be available in starting a new church." He had $1,057. He paid a $17 water bill, $40 for groceries, and gave $1,000 to the church. Henson did not tell his wife or anyone else. God moved a couple to Thomas Road Baptist Church, close friends Henson now calls "Mom and Pop Morris," who felt led to help a student through school. They invited the Hensons to move into their home, giving them a place to live without rent, plus helping them purchase food. He figures that the Morrises gave him more than $7,000 worth of rent and groceries, seven times the amount he had given to God.

Al Henson graduated from the University of Tennessee. He was living in Gallatin when he felt God calling him into full-time Christian service. He remembers walking to the back porch of his house and looking out over a section of the city. "God gave me a burden for the city and I know he has called me to reach all of Nashville for Christ."

After finishing his classwork at the seminary in December of 1977, Henson moved to Nashville. He had prayed for this church for three years while in seminary. He testified, "I did not have a problem with what to do after graduation. I knew God was leading me to Nashville." He rented an apartment in Bavaria Apartments, with the stipulation that he could use the recreation room to start a church. He and his wife, and associate Ken Collins, knocked on three thousand doors the first month.

On the first Sunday, 41 showed up. Nila Miller professed Christ that day and is still a member of the church. That evening, 19 people came back for the evening service. Inasmuch as many relatives were there for the first Sunday, Al figured there were at the first service about 20 people interested in starting a church. Because of their hard work, 38 people were present the second Sunday and 43 the third.

When the church was only two months old, Henson passed twenty-five acres on I-24 not far from the apartment building. "As I drove past and saw the tenement house, I knew the property could be purchased." When first contacted, the owner refused because he planned to will the property to his daughter. When Henson called on the owner a second time, he was told "No!" emphatically. Henson walked the property line and prayed for the tract of land. On several occasions he returned with his wife and knelt on the property and asked God to give it to him. He believed (by interventional faith) that God would give the land to the church.

Finally, for three days Henson fasted and prayed that God would touch the owner's heart. He got the church to pray for the property. Then he visited the man and shared his burden for reaching the city of Nashville. As he left, he asked the owner, "Will you pray about selling the property to us?" The man's wife said, "I'll see that he prays about it."

The next day the man phoned Henson and said, "The Lord spoke to me as I have never had him speak to me before; I know that God wants you to have this property." Then the owner went on, "If you will come up with $29,000, I will loan you the other $71,000 to buy the property." The church was given ninety days to raise the down payment on the mortgage that was pegged at 9 percent interest.

Slowly some money came in. Six days before the deadline, the church had raised only $5,000. A Christian friend, Melcolm Barrett, not a member of the church, told Henson, "I have been listening to you on the radio." He invited Henson, "Let's get on our knees and pray about this money." After praying, he said, "Come by tomorrow and I will get $24,000 for the property." He loaned the church the money at no interest for an indefinite period. According to Henson, this was one of the greatest miracles in the life of the church.

Henson says that a pastor's wife also helps in building a church. During the construction of the first building, the ladies of the church gave $38,000. His wife gave her engagement ring. Because of her example, many ladies in the congregation gave sacrificially. Out of that sense of sacrifice, God prospered the church and gave the people their first building.

The church began construction on a 30′ × 75′ metal building that would seat 225 in services. An old home on the property was used for Sunday school. On October 27, 1978, they moved into the metal building and averaged 160 that first year.

The growth of Lighthouse Baptist Church is even more significant when, according to Henson, "Our crowd is a drive-in crowd; we do not have a bus ministry." The church has fifty to sixty men who are trained soul-winners. The church does not have a regular weekly visitation program, but wins souls throughout the week.

When Henson went to Nashville, he did not pray for hundreds. "I prayed for one family a week." During that first year, 53 families joined the church. As a matter of fact, everyone prayed for a family a week to join the church. Sometimes when a family visited the church, someone said to them, "You're the family we have been praying for."

In talking of his leadership, Henson testifies, "I am a man of sacrifice and I have led my people to sacrifice." Then he went on to state, "I believe there are over twenty-five men who would sell their houses for their Lord." He testifies that the church has grown "because I have taught the people in the area of sacrificial living."

FAITH IS SUPERNATURAL INTERVENTION

Al Henson defined faith as "allowing God to move supernaturally into a situation." From that definition he explained, "Faith is determining what is God's will, then trusting him to carry out his will."

When Henson was faced with the three possibilities of faith: (1) instrumental, (2) insightful, and (3) interventional, he said, "Faith is interventional because that means it is miraculous or supernatural." In a letter to the students at Liberty, Henson explains, "I consider living by faith . . . a necessary way of life, whether it be personally or in a ministry. Faith is not a passive thing, but rather faith is operating under circumstances in which we shall fail without God's intervention."

When Henson was asked to explain what he meant by "intervention," he explained, "What God orders, he supplies. If it is God's will for the church to go forward, we can trust him to overcome any barriers or to supply any need."

Henson said, "When I accept Jesus Christ by faith, he becomes real to me. When I accept the Holy Spirit by faith, he fills me. When I obey the Lord Jesus Christ by faith, he manifests himself through me." To explain this, Henson said, "Faith is the supernatural manifestation of Jesus Christ in a life."

When Henson was asked where he got his faith, he said that it comes from God: "I do not pray for faith—it is the gift of God. Rather, I pray that this gift might become more manifested in my life."

Henson believes that, as the church has grown, so

his faith has grown. Henson testifies that there are several means by which faith grows.

First, I daily ask God to pour his faith through my life. Second, the more I know about Jesus Christ and the Bible, the more I can trust him. Hence, more faith can be manifested by fellowshiping with Jesus Christ and drawing upon the principles of the Bible. In the third place, my faith grows in its manifestation as I take a step of faith. God does not manifest faith in our lives just because we ask him to. Faith is manifested more when it is exercised.

Henson illustrates the growth of faith with the verse, "From faith to faith" (Rom. 1:17). He interprets this verse to mean a person could grow from weak faith to strong faith.

A. *Faith and location.* When Henson was asked to relate how faith led him to Nashville, he indicated there was never a question in his mind that he was to minister there.

From the moment I went onto the back porch and saw Nashville, I knew that God wanted me to come to this city. I knew that God wanted me to do more than just build one church; God wanted us to plant several churches in the Nashville area and make an impact on this city for God.

B. *Faith and doctrine.* Henson noted, "Obviously a person has no faith if he does not believe and accept the person of the Lord Jesus Christ." Then he went on to say that, "If a person believes in the lordship of Christ, and he attempts to live by faith, the unseen minor doctrinal faults would not stop God from manifesting himself." Henson said that God will always work in a person's life to purify his doctrine. He believes that the gift of faith comes before pure doctrine, because faith is in the person of Christ. But, he was quick to add, saving faith is based on biblical doctrine. In relating the two, he said they run full-cycle. Doctrine is first, which explains saving faith; then a Christian's exercise of faith purifies his doctrine. "If a person seeks God with all his heart, God will purify his faith, and his faith will purify his doctrine."

Henson believes one of the problems among independent Baptists is that they do not see the necessity to grow in faith. He sees many who understand the doctrine but have not grown beyond that understanding. He feels many Christians "do not know how to walk in faith."

C. *Faith and objectives.* Henson believes that the purpose of the church is to bring glory to God. He sees the purpose of the church to be "conformed to the image" of Jesus Christ (Rom. 8:29). The objective found in Matthew 28:19 and 20 grows out of this purpose. The objective of the church is: (1) evangelism, (2) discipleship, (3) fellowship, and (4) worship. He believes the Great Commission is given to the church, but is not carried out until people are made into disciples and are walking in conformity to the image of Jesus Christ.

When I came to Nashville I did not think we would grow, although I was concerned about growth. I determined that I would disciple people and cause them to grow in Jesus Christ. I found many people in the city who were hungry for the Word of God. People came to the church because of the message and the fellowship of the service. This has been the predominant cause of our church growth.

To explain this, Henson indicated that 25 percent is new-convert growth, 50 percent of the growth is from Christians who are not from another church, and 25 percent is transfer growth.

D. *Faith and principles.* Henson believes faith comes before the fullness and power of the Holy Spirit. The promise of being filled with the Holy Spirit is faith and not works. Then when a person is filled with the Spirit, he can build a church that will glorify the Lord. Henson said that he determined in seminary, "I will accomplish more by becoming a man of God than I will by just learning principles and methodology." He noted, "The blessing of God is not upon a place or principles, but rather upon his man."

He challenges students at Liberty, "When you are properly positioned in relationship with God, he will bless you. You shall prosper and your ministry shall be a success in God's eyes, no matter what part of the world you are in."

Henson determined to walk with God, but he also determined that he would not neglect principles and methods. He feels that too many have emphasized principles and techniques but have neglected the spiritual walk with God.

When it comes to understanding principles of saturation evangelism, or any other principles, Henson believes that certain methods will work only in certain cities. "The man of God must have wisdom to apply methods to the situation." Henson believes that church busing will work in some cities, but he did not use it in Nashville. At times in his ministry he has used Sunday school campaigns, but his church has also grown without using campaigns. He indicated that certain techniques reach a certain kind of people, while other techniques reach a different kind of people. When he emphasized preaching the Word and helping people to experience the fullness of the Spirit, he attracted a different type of person to the church, people of a more serious mind about Christ and his kingdom.

When asked to explain the gift of faith, Henson indicated that "Every Christian manifests some aspect of the gift of faith because every Christian has Jesus Christ in his heart." Then he went on to specify, "The gift of faith is the ability to live and to teach other people to live by that same kind of faith." In keeping with that explanation he states, "I have the gift of faith, because God has used me to motivate others to live by faith; but my greatest gift is exhortation." Henson believes that "if a man has the gift of faith, others can learn of faith as they watch this gift being manifested."

To illustrate this example of faith, some time later, Al Henson stopped taking a salary from the church. He announced on only one occasion to the congregation that he was going to live by faith. He did this because of the criticism he heard in Nashville that many ministers were preaching for money. He did not want his salary to be a reproach to the gospel.

Two weeks after he went off salary, one of the members placed an offering box near the rear door where people could place gifts for their pastor. Henson testified, "I could not have lived on the money that was put in the box, but God supplied my needs from others outside of this local church." Henson does not take money from the box; another man receives it and places it into an account, along with the gifts that are given directly to Henson. If there is anything extra in the account, it is given to meet other needs in the church. Recently, the excess was used as a down payment on a house for one of the staff members. Henson has been criticized because people are not provided with a receipt for income tax credit. However, the person who oversees the account issues receipts. This way, the church is accountable to IRS examination.

When asked what was the biggest experience of faith in his life, Henson indicated his receiving

$29,000 in ninety days. As soon as he said this, Henson explained, "The early steps of faith that I took are not as big by today's perspective, but they were big then."

CONCLUSION

Of all the church planters in this study, in his view of faith, Al Henson is closest to Jerry Falwell. Both say that faith is interventional and have demonstrated that God can intervene in a crisis situation to solve problems that have blocked church growth. Al Henson seems to have brought his attitude toward faith with him to Liberty, where it was amplified.

It is obvious that success in trusting God to solve one problem leads to a greater trust when succeeding problems face the ministry. It seems that when Henson first planted the church, he gave more attention to applying the principles of super-aggressive evangelism (he visited 3,000 homes to start the church). Now, Henson seems to give more attention to nurturing his people and emphasizing the Spirit-filled life. Apparently, as he once trusted God to intervene for evangelistic growth, he now centers on a ministry of communicating faith and the Spirit-filled life.

3
HERITAGE
BAPTIST CHURCH
Lynchburg, Virginia
Rod Kidd, Pastor

Most Liberty graduates think that Lynchburg would be one of the most difficult places to begin a church. Due to the widespread influence of Dr. Jerry Falwell and the Thomas Road Baptist Church, they felt a high level of competition would exist, or that they would have few opportunities or lack distinctiveness in their ministries. Yet Rod Kidd, a graduate of Liberty Baptist Seminary, has led Heritage Baptist Church from a humble start in the basement of a home, through the construction of a large building, to an approximate 400 in attendance today. Located less than five miles from Thomas Road Baptist Church, the church is identified as a fundamentalist congregation (as is Thomas Road), yet Heritage has developed its unique identity with emphasis on Bible teaching and a warm family spirit.

Heritage Baptist Church began when several families left another church in Lynchburg, Virginia, because they felt it had departed from some biblical principles. They did not want to split the church, yet they wanted to deal with the matter scripturally; therefore, they went to the pastor and church officials with the problem. When nothing was done, the families left quietly. When they met one another while shopping or on other business, they found out that none of them had joined another church. So they met together in the basement of one of their homes. Most of them agreed to meet again within thirty days to determine if they would join a church or if they should begin a church. That was November 1976. The church began meeting in December, and Dr. Robert Hughes, then dean of Liberty Baptist Seminary, served as interim pastor. He gave the young congregation a solid doctrinal foundation, and Dr. Frank Schmitt, professor of Christian Education at Liberty Baptist Seminary, helped the church write a constitution.

When Dr. Hughes went out of town on a preaching mission, he invited Rod Kidd, a freshman at the seminary, to preach to the infant congregation. The small church liked Rod Kidd and asked him to come back as a candidate. When he did, they called him as their pastor. The question has been asked whether Rod is the founder of the church. Dr. Hughes had said, "I do not want to be your pastor; I just want to help you get started." Technically, Rod Kidd is the first pastor. Some see him as the founder, since the church was in the same condition when he came in June 1977 as when they began meeting.

According to Kidd, the first step of faith was to get the church to move out of the basement. The occasion was a church fellowship meeting to which Rod Kidd refers as the "swimming pool meeting." While the ladies were inside, Rod Kidd came outside and saw the men sitting around the swimming pool. He could tell from their conversation that it was serious. They were discussing whether or not the church should continue. Kidd was apprehensive about joining the conversation. The men expressed concern that the church did not have deacons, plus several other matters. Their greatest concern was the lack of a building. Out of that meeting, the men took greater responsibility for the church, and Kidd realized that they had to move out of the basement. In a great step of faith, the church rented an abandoned convenience-store building on Lakeside Drive. It was a great financial commitment, but God honored it and the church went forward.

Kidd said, "Just continuing the church from week to week was a step of faith." In the infant church, only one person made a profession of faith (during six months), and Rod felt this was "terrible . . . just terrible, because we needed conversions as an affirmation of our purpose."

While meeting in the convenience store, the church took its next major step of faith. The people voted to enter a bond program to raise money for the present building. The step of faith involved selling $125,000 in bonds. Rod admitted, "I was scared to death." He had seen other churches go into a bond program and fail to sell their bonds. Kidd knew that if the church did not sell its bonds, the consequences would be so dire they might endanger the church's existence.

He also indicated that they did several things against the advice of professional bond salesmen. First, they gave low interest rates; they did not want people to buy the bonds simply for the sake of profit. Also, they sold the bonds before they had them in hand. Finally, they were told not to buy the property because it was on a dead-end street. However, the church has visibility from the expressway and the property has become an outstanding location. The bonds were sold on time and the church constructed its new facilities. God honored their commitment, and the church jumped 70 a week in attendance when it moved into the new facilities. Again the next year, the church grew by another 70 in average weekly attendance.

When the church constructed its new facilities, they

had wisely provided for a basement. When they first occupied the facilities, the basement was not complete, so it was not usable. The first expansion involved renovating the basement. Next, the auditorium was expanded by taking out classrooms.

Soon after they occupied the building, the church planned an attendance campaign called "Friend Day." When they were averaging 84 in attendance, an attendance goal of 100 was twice missed while they still met in the convenience store. In the new facilities, the Friend Day campaign challenged everyone to bring a friend, without setting a goal of 100. However, attendance jumped from an average 84 to 237 on that day. Even though not a large number of people professed salvation that day, Friend Day did something to the corporate attitude of the church. They lost their "storefront mentality" and became "successful" in their own eyes. They realized they could attract their friends to their church. Subsequently, many have professed salvation, and other Christians have moved their membership into the church. Since then, the church has sponsored annual fall and spring campaigns to reach the lost for salvation and to bring unchurched people into the church.

FAITH IS VISION OF WHAT GOD CAN DO THROUGH YOU

Rod Kidd was asked with which of the three concepts of faith he agreed, (1) instrumental, (2) insightful, or (3) interventional. He replied that "Faith is having a vision of what God can do and trusting him to do it through you." Kidd indicates that when he had a vision of a church on Breezewood Drive, by faith he saw what could be accomplished. Then he trusted God to give him the ability to sell the bonds and lead the church to construct the building. Kidd expresses his faith through the Word of God (instrumental) and by having a vision of what God can do (insight). Rod Kidd does not define faith as great interventions.

Kidd said he did not think he had the gift of faith, especially compared to a giant like Dr. Falwell.

Asked how his faith has grown, Kidd said, "I do not think I can grow faith by myself; faith is both a gift of God and something to be nurtured by obedience." He added, "Faith is a miraculous mixture of both." He said if he is faithful in trusting God for little things, God will open greater things for him. He explained that he would not take credit for cultivating his faith; but he realizes it is his responsibility to carry out the duties that God has for him. "When I am faithful, God increases my faith to trust him for greater things."

A. *Faith and Location.* Pastoring in Lynchburg was a big step of faith to Rod Kidd. "I had to answer two questions," he noted. "First, I had to determine if Lynchburg needed another church." Kidd knew there were many lost in the area. Also, through his witnessing, he knew there were some who would not be reached by Thomas Road Baptist Church (his church before his call to Heritage). That question answered, he faced a second one. "Does God want me in Lynchburg?" He answered that, after he preached, he knew God was calling him to Lynchburg and that the Lord would bless him there.

B. *Faith and doctrine.* When Rod Kidd was asked to relate his faith to doctrine, he stated, "I know that God honors his Word and that those who preach biblical doctrine are blessed of God." Yet when viewing those who have different doctrine, Kidd noted, "I think that Presbyterians, Church of God members, and others can have faith and be blessed of God. I know of men who disagree with me in doctrine yet they are my heroes in the faith. They defend the faith and they are men of God."

Rod feels that God blesses faith, even when a person has wrong expressions of the personal faith. But Kidd is quick to maintain that a man must not deny the essentials of Christianity. "I feel that many times God blesses us despite ourselves. We may hold to some small item that is wrong, but when God wants to do something and our heart is basically right, then God blesses our faith and causes his church to prosper."

C. *Faith and objectives.* The purpose of the church is to carry out the Great Commission. Kidd says he will win souls, baptize them, and teach them the Word of God. Because he is located in Lynchburg, many people ask how large the church will become. He answers, "My goal is not to be a second Thomas Road. I have a goal to reach 1,000 in attendance." When he looks at the multiple ministry of Thomas Road, Kidd says he will not try to begin a Christian school or a camp. "We can use what they make available to us."

By faith, Kidd sees a family church with emphasis on a teaching ministry. In keeping with his view of faith, he is trusting God to help him carry out that vision.

D. *Faith and principles.* Kidd is committed to the principles that were taught to him at Liberty. He notes a distinction between principles and application. As an illustration: the principle is reaching people for Christ, the application is using the bus ministry. He says he will not use an application that is ineffective. He sees Thomas Road doing an excellent task of saturating Lynchburg, so, "We are having a difficult time in the bus ministry." Since Kidd believes faith is vision, he has faith/vision that Heritage can reach families. So in the fall of 1982, they sponsored "Discovery Day" and contacted 13,000 homes. Although the attendance was not as great as expected, on each succeeding Sunday new families visited the church.

Kidd is concerned about students who go out of Liberty with great vision that is not realistic. He noted that

Dr. Falwell had 864 on his first anniversary, so most Liberty students expect to do the same thing. "When a student does not have 864 on his first anniversary, he thinks he is a failure." Kidd said, "I had to adjust to reality." Kidd said that he has to minister by faith through his "dry season" when people are not being saved, as well as through the times when God "opens the windows of heaven and many are saved." He remembers the example of the fall Sunday school campaign and Rally Day. He trusted God for a great number of people to make professions of faith. He had trained counselors to be ready to pray with those who came forward for salvation. Follow-up material was printed and the entire church was ready for a great harvest of souls. But no one professed salvation that day. "I was discouraged," said Kidd. "But if I had had the long look, I would have seen what God was doing. For several weeks after Rally Day, we had three to five people profess salvation each week."

Rod Kidd noted,

Every once in awhile I have taken giant steps of faith that have absolutely engulfed me. I was terrified and I never wanted to do it again. But because of the burden to serve Jesus Christ, I took the risk, and God answered prayer. Now I am stronger. As I look back on those terrifying experiences, I do not want to take them again. But because of my call to the ministry, I know that I will step out in faith many times in the future.

CONCLUSION

Rod Kidd believes faith is vision (insight) that motivates a minister to make correct decisions based on the Word of God (instrumental) to build the church. He has led the church to take two steps of faith (larger than usual) that resulted in growth (obviously, other

steps of faith were taken, but these two are correlated
to empirical results). The steps of faith were the move
into the convenience store building and construction
of new facilities.

Kidd has a faith/vision of what he wants to accomplish in Lynchburg. His faith is tied to Scripture (fulfilling the Great Commission) and to the contextual
factors of the community. He knows that Thomas Road
is a factor that affects his church, yet his faith/vision
involves a type of church that will adapt to a family and
teaching ministry which will appeal to the section of
Lynchburg he wants to reach for Christ.

4
HOLY MOUNTAIN BAPTIST CHURCH
Kingsport, Tennessee
Steve Ray, Pastor

Steve Ray was twenty-three years old when he graduated from Liberty Bible Institute and returned home to Kingsport, Tennessee, to plant Holy Mountain Baptist Church, June 27, 1976. He is the youngest of the Liberty graduates mentioned in this book, yet he has led his church to the third largest attendance of the Liberty graduates. After six years, the church has assets of $500,000 and an annual income of $264,000 with per capita income of $6.64.

While a student at Liberty Bible Institute, Steve Ray knew he was going to start a church, but the question was where. He confessed, "I was willing to go anywhere and start a church," and had even contemplated going to New England. He said, "My wife had promised to be a missionary, so I knew that she would go with me anywhere."

Each time he returned home to the tri-city area, he said that he got a burden between Bristol and Kingsport, primarily because he did not know of an aggressive church reaching the entire area. Confronted with the possibility that his feeling was homesickness or nostalgia, he replied, "I know the difference between

God's voice and homesickness." Then one night in bed, he got a distinct burden that God wanted him to start a church in Kingsport, his hometown. "It was not an audible voice, but I knew God wanted me in Kingsport." He had been memorizing and meditating on the verse, "Trust in the Lord with all thine heart; and lean not unto thine own understanding. In all thy ways acknowledge him, and he shall direct thy paths" (Prov. 3:5, 6). Immediately, he put all of his trust in God and knew that God would guide him to the exact place he should go.

Two weeks later, Steve visited Kingsport and decided to minister to the entire city (not just one section of the area); therefore he chose to start in the middle of the city. With that in mind, he went to a middle school (grades six to eight) on Ross and Randlett Streets in city-center and asked the principal for permission to rent the facilities. The principal replied, "No! We do not rent the building."

"God told me to start a church in this school," Steve told the principal. He just laughed, but did promise to check into renting the building. He gave Steve no assurance it could be done. The next time Steve came to Kingsport, the principal had talked with the janitor, who was willing to open the building on Sunday. So they agreed on $300 rent per month.

Steve Ray set the budget for the new church at $1,150 per month, $200 a week for a salary, and $300 for rent of the facilities. When he arrived at Kingsport, he knew God would provide for his finances, so he did not go to work or ask other churches to underwrite him.

The first great step of faith for the church revolved around the first service. He publicly told everyone he was praying for 100 people to attend the first service. Several told him not to get his hopes up too high.

He got the school building ready and planned to begin at 10:30 A.M. on Sunday, June 27, 1976. The service was to be in the gymnasium. Young Steve Ray stood in the balcony overlooking the empty chairs at 10:25 and counted only 18 people there. He went into a private room and prayed no more than five minutes. He testified, "I prayed like I lived, 'total belief.' " He prayed, "Lord, I asked and claimed that you would send in 100 people, then I have gone out and worked for them. Now send them in." He said, "When I went to the front door, it was like a mountain stream of people pouring in the front door; 119 were present for that first service."

According to Ray, getting the people there was a great step of faith, but trusting God for the money was not a great step of faith. "I was not worried about money, and it was not even a challenge to my faith to pray for money. I knew that God had led me to Kingsport and I knew that he would provide the money." For the two weeks prior to starting the church, he went visiting door to door, inviting people to come to the church. Many people gave him money to start the church. One lady who later became a member of the church gave him $1,000, another $300. A total of over $2,500 was received for the church from free gifts, even before the church began. "God has always taken care of my need before I asked," he said.

The next great step of faith involved the purchase of ground. During the first six months of the church, average attendance was 76. The pastor told the church, after finding eight acres of ground, "This is the place where God wants us." He tramped through the bushes looking at the ground, until he came to a graceful weeping willow tree. Kneeling at its base, Steve Ray claimed the land for Holy Mountain Baptist Church. "That tree," he told the people, "is the very place where the church's front steps will be."

He shared the vision of the willow tree with his people. The price of the property was $48,000 and the church was given four weeks to raise $10,750 for a down payment. He remembers someone telling him, "You are getting ready to destroy your church by this step of faith." But Steve Ray challenged the people to believe in "the God of the impossible." He placed a large thermometer in front of the school gymnasium. At the end of two weeks only $900 had come in. Steve Ray confessed to discouragement. He decided to go door to door and ask for money. He canvassed the area asking for money for the down payment on the property. By the end of the week, he had raised $6,950. (When someone told him it was not biblical to ask the unsaved for money, he replied, "It is biblical to ask people to give for God and I did it.") Then he went to the church and reported that they had approximately $7,800 ($6,950 plus $900). He took an offering, which made a total of $10,754; that was $4.88 over their goal.

The church met for the next two years in the school gym before moving into the permanent location. To build on the new property, the church borrowed $100,000 and the men of the church began working on the new location. Ray felt the men who volunteered to donate their labor were not as zealous as they had been in promising. This produced a great crisis in his faith. He testified, "One Saturday, I had to make a hospital visit and I left the men working. When I got back they had not done a thing—they were just sitting there waiting for me." This discouraged him. He took a one-week missionary trip to Costa Rica; when he returned he found that the men had made absolutely no progress on the building, despite their promise to him.

"I am going to quit," he told his wife. He felt that the job was too big for him and he wanted to go someplace else to start a church. That night as he tried to sleep, God spoke to him. "I did not hear a voice, but I knew God said, 'No!'" Steve Ray went on to say, "But I could not run. God had put me there and I had to finish the church." The church finished the building in 1978, two years after Ray started the work.

Speaking about taking a step of faith, Ray said, "Do not look at your bank account but at the command of God." The church wanted to purchase two buses for $2,800. Steve prayed, and the following Sunday morning between Sunday school and church, a man gave him a check for $1,000 (to make up for tithes that he had not been giving to the church). Another person handed him a check for $2,100, a total of $3,100. Steve said that the church bought the buses for $2,800 and had them painted for $300, the exact cost of $3,100. The buses represented a way to win souls.

"We should never worry about God's meeting our needs if we are winning souls," says Ray. As Towns interviewed him for this chapter, Ray showed him a check for $500. "I just won a man to the Lord thirty minutes ago and he gave me this $500 check for the church."

Another step of faith was when the church added salaried employees. In 1978, the church was spending the same amount of money that it received. Steve estimated that an additional $1,100 per month was needed to hire a music director. The money was not available, but he knew God wanted him to expand the staff. When he found the right man, he hired him; automatically, church giving jumped $1,100 per month.

"There was no fund-raising program or vote to expand the budget. We stepped out on faith and God brought the money in." Steve Ray was asked, "Suppose the money did not come in after you hired the staff member?" He responded, "I never thought that way; I knew the money would come in." He was then asked, "Suppose the people had opposed the expansion?" He responded, "It was God's will, and that is what they wanted." Steve Ray won't admit the possibility of failure when he believes God is leading him in a step of faith.

Each year, the church gives a birthday offering to the Lord. On the night after Thanksgiving, the church has a banquet and takes a cash gift for missions. In 1976, they set a goal of $6,000 and $7,500 was received. Still another year, they set a goal of $20,000 and $21,237 came in on one evening.

FAITH IS MOUNTAIN-MOVING ABILITY

When asked to define faith, Steve Ray said, "Faith is mountain-moving ability." Facing the three alternatives that faith is (1) instrumental, (2) insightful, and (3) interventional, Steve Ray said faith is definitely interventional. He testifies that mountain-moving faith is the basis of the rapid growth of Holy Mountain Baptist Church.

To Steve Ray, the gift of faith is believing God for an answer that you cannot see, then praying to remove the barriers to the work of God. He went on to say, "There is a fine line between little faith and great faith." By that he means, "All Christians have little faith, but a few people have the gift of faith that is mountain-moving faith." When asked how he got his gift of faith, he testified, "I ask and pray for faith beyond my years."

"What is the biggest thing you will trust God for in the future?" he was asked. But Steve Ray refused to be drawn into speculations on matters not presently possible. He did not want to talk in terms of four or five thousand in church attendance. He said, "The biggest step of faith in the future will be to build an auditorium to seat 1,800." Asked why he did not take a step of faith for a 5,000-seat auditorium, he replied,

"I do not need an auditorium that will seat 5,000, but I need an auditorium that will seat 1,800." Then, with the maturity of an older faith, he said, "God only gives us faith to trust him for what we need, not for our empty speculation."

In reply to a query about the source of his faith, Steve indicated that at Thomas Road Baptist Church he took notes on everything, not just in classes. "I watched Jerry Falwell do everything, with a view of following his example." Then Steve Ray testified that 90 percent of his faith had been caught from the vision and faith of Jerry Falwell. He also mentioned others at Liberty, such as Ken Chapman, Associate Dean of the (now) Institute of Biblical Studies, and Grant Rice, a church planter from Chicago whose faith had encouraged him to start Holy Mountain Baptist Church.

He also traces the growth of his faith back to his call into full-time Christian service. He had a good job in Kingsport, in the General Shale Brick and Block plant, when he felt that God was calling him to preach. Several people counseled him against going to school, indicating that he would lose his burden and zeal. Many in the church he attended were against ministerial education. Someone told him, "If God has called you to preach, you do not need to go to school—just preach." Going against the well-meant advice of friends was to him a fearful step of faith. "I knew God wanted me to go to Liberty, but I did not want to go against my friends."

A. *Faith and location.* Steve Ray says that faith is involved in everything that builds a church, even finding the right location. He believes faith is interventional. God intervened to call him back to Kingsport and God has intervened to keep him at Kingsport (when he tried to leave but could not).

Steve Ray did not identify his faith with vision or insight. When the history of the church is examined,

Ray does not speak of a long-range vision of large numbers or a complete church/campus complex. As described above, he stated he could only trust God for present needs, such as an 1,800-seat auditorium.

B. *Faith and doctrine.* When asked to correlate faith to doctrine, Ray answers he is absolutely sure that what he preaches is correct. "I agree with what I read in the Bible, and that is what I preach." The tie between his faith and doctrine is reflected in the sincerity of his approach to doctrine. Asked to rank the role of faith in the growth of churches, especially those that disagree with his doctrine, Steve Ray answered, "Every time a man preaches the Bible, there will be some growth." He went on to explain: "The church that is closer to the Word of God will have more growth."

C. *Faith and objectives.* To Steve Ray, the purpose of the church is to reach and win souls, carrying out the Great Commission. To him, the purpose of the church and faith go hand in hand; a person carries out the Great Commission by faith.

D. *Faith and principles.* Ray says he had to learn how to apply the principles of evangelism to faith so he could attract a crowd. He stated, "I had to go out and knock on doors, applying the principles of reaching people; then I prayed that God would touch their hearts and motivate them to come to church." He understands and applies the correlation between faith and principles. The application of super-aggressive evangelism is just as imperative as the application of faith in God. "To apply the right principles and to apply faith is the same thing," he said.

To most people taking a step of faith, there is always a threat of failure. Therefore, putting one's faith in God is more than a passive action. It is active, involving the total person—intellect, emotion, and will. The act of faith overcomes fear when the person has confidence that God will not fail. Steve Ray testifies that trusting God for money did not give him a fear of failure. He knew the need would be met. But applying the principles of church growth exercised his faith to the stretching point.

In discussing the growth of faith, Steve Ray says, "Things that used to be big steps are no longer big steps of faith." He mentioned that when he trusted God for $48,000 for property, that was a staggering step of faith; but it would not be a big step of faith today. "Massive steps of the past seem small now, and the steps that are massive today will one day in the future be small."

CONCLUSION

Steve Ray has exercised his faith to intervene in the crisis and barriers that attempted to stop the growth of his church. The faith demonstrated by Jerry Falwell was also used by Steve Ray to plant and build Holy Mountain Baptist Church. Whereas some Liberty graduates are measured and rational in expressing their faith, Steve Ray seems to forsake caution and take risks that he interprets as "steps of faith."

5
WACHUSETT VALLEY BAPTIST CHURCH
Holden, Massachusetts
John Martelli, Pastor

John Martelli almost lost his life in Vietnam and came home in a wheelchair, paralyzed from his waist down. He was not bitter at God because of his incapacity, but was grateful to be alive. He came to know Christ and was trained at Liberty Baptist College. He was not sure what he could do for God until he preached at the funeral of his brother. Twelve persons made professions of faith at the funeral from among members of his family and friends who were Roman Catholic. More people made decisions for Christ at the graveside service. This convinced Martelli to return to his hometown, Holden, Massachusetts, to plant Wachusett Valley Baptist Church. After five years, the church owns fifty acres of land and is worth $350,000. Weekly attendance averages 130 persons and the church has a vision of reaching the entire valley.

Since the history of many new churches is wrapped up in the history of the church planter, an analysis of the life and conversion of John Martelli is needed to understand the development of the church. He grew up in a Roman Catholic home and as a young man married his childhood sweetheart. It appeared that everything was going well for him; but then his life seemed to fall apart in Vietnam. He fell with shrapnel wounds when an army building was shelled by enemy rockets. The building caught fire. In his initial anger, he wanted to kill the enemy. Five seconds later a second rocket hit the building. This time his injuries were critical. He felt sure that he would die, but he managed to crawl out of the building. He lay on the ground, where his unit was pinned down with small-arms fire. Another soldier picked him up and carried him through a second burning building to a medical area. He testified, "After the second rocket, I was never angry at the enemy for my being paralyzed. I was simply grateful to God that I was alive. The God I had known as a Roman Catholic had protected me and I was grateful."

He came home from Vietnam in a wheelchair, paralyzed from the waist down. One day, months later, he saw his toes moving but he could not feel them, because he had no feeling in his legs. Based on that optimistic development, he applied for physical therapy, after which limited sensitivity and mobility returned to his legs. Today, he walks on braces and wears special shoes provided by the government.

Back in Holden, Massachusetts, Martelli operated his auto repair garage and sought to reestablish life with his wife and family. Marsha began attending a gospel-preaching church where she made a profession of faith in Christ as her personal Savior. John testified, "Her godly walk was a testimony to me." He knew she was right and his own life was empty. His drinking and minor drug addiction (a by-product of hospitalization) proved to him that his childhood religion had nothing to offer him. He went to his wife's church with her, and the first time he heard the gospel he knew the message was true. "No one had ever told me that Jesus saves, and I immediately wanted him to save me."

After conversion, John Martelli attended Liberty Baptist College, studying in the pastoral major program. He did not know where God wanted him to spend his life in ministry. During his last year in college, his older brother was killed in a construction accident, and John called his father, suggesting, "Do not have a Catholic funeral; let me come home and preach the funeral."

The fact that they allowed him to perform the funeral was evidence that God was at work in Holden. (When he went away to college, his family had called him a "turncoat.") He testified, "God supported me as I preached my brother's funeral. During the invitation twelve people professed salvation. At the graveside, still other people came to know Jesus Christ." At the funeral he had simply given his testimony and told people that "Jesus saves." Until then, he had not wanted to return to Holden and start a church because his reputation in the community was so poor. However, the funeral experience indicated that he was called of God to Holden, "like a neon sign, calling me home." (The first day he returned to Holden, he led Jimmy Santanaw, a boyhood friend, to Jesus Christ.)

John Martelli admitted he knew little about how to start a church, although he was greatly motivated by Jerry Falwell. He began by taking a religious survey of the area. The results of the survey further indicated that he should begin in Holden.

Not knowing how to begin, he "prayed and stumbled." He explained that he started a Bible study in his home on Wednesday evenings. After two weeks, he realized this was not the way to start a church. He felt the people who came to Bible study were only interested in Christian fellowship. Martelli realized that he needed to start a church with a soul-winning emphasis, not just a Bible study. So he found a building that had been used by a lodge, agreed upon a price, and began meetings in September 1978. Twelve came to the first service. At the end of the sermon, he gave an invitation to come forward for salvation and/or join the church. All 12 people came forward and joined the church; those not previously saved became Christians. The church grew through soul-winning during that year. On the first anniversary, there were 45 in attendance.

At the end of the second year, the town took over the lodge from the owners on an "imminent domain" basis. Martelli knew that "if the church did not have a building, I could not hold the people." He had been praying seriously for a permanent building even before they had to move. The postman who delivered mail on Bullard Street had made a profession of faith and joined the church. He told Martelli about fifty acres that were for sale, with an old farmhouse and bakery. The asking price was $190,000. At the time, the church had only $500 in the bank. No one had told Martelli to begin a building fund account. Martelli began praying about the land. When he went to see the owner, she testified that her mother, an officer in the Salvation Army, had prayed that God would someday use the property for the work of God. The owner agreed to sell the property for $130,000. But Martelli could find no one to finance the purchase of the ground; $500 was far from enough. As he prayed with the church, the mailman agreed to sell his house, for which he received $45,000. He gave $30,000 to the church, with the understanding that he would live in the farmhouse. Another man in the church gave $35,000, which made enough to finance a 50 percent down payment. In addition, the people raised $5,000 that allowed them to renovate the bakery facilities for the church. Martelli sees this step of faith as rewarded by God through financial provision.

There was a second aspect to this step of faith. Martelli knew that God wanted him to start a Christian school. He announced this to the church after they had lost their lodge building but did not yet have the bakery. They started the Christian school in the fall of 1980 with 24 students, with no building. Martelli indicated he had no doubts about the venture, though the men of the church (the church had no deacons) did not understand and were reluctant to back him in the step of faith. So the pastor began the Christian school in his home, using his living room, den, basement, and dining room. "There was no Christian school within thirty miles, and I could not travel that far twice daily. I would not allow my children to go back to public schools because of the ungodly influence."

Martelli testified, "By the eyes of faith I could see what we were supposed to do, but I could not see how it could be accomplished. So I simply obeyed God and began the school in my home." The men of the church did not oppose it, they just did not at first support it financially.

The school met for two months in the pastor's house, while God was providing fifty acres of ground and the bakery building. Martelli says, "If I had not stepped out in faith and begun the school, I am not sure that God would have provided $65,000 for the property." He went on to say, "If a man will do the will of God by faith, God will reward his obedience."

When asked if he had entertained doubts about getting the building, Martelli answered, "I had no doubts that God wanted me to do it. I had doubts about my ability to raise the money and to find the location."

FAITH LOOKS BACKWARD AND FORWARD

When John Martelli was asked to define faith he said, "Faith has eyes on both sides of its head. It looks backward to see what God has done, then looks within to see what God is saying, and finally looks forward to see the future." Martelli went on to describe, "Faith sees what God would have a man do, then the man steps out in faith (not blind faith) based on what God has done in the past." When faced with the three alternatives of faith (1. instrumental, 2. insightful, and 3. interventional), Martelli says that faith is vision or insight. He testifies, "All I have to do is to see what God wants to do, and I will try to do it." On one occasion, Martelli sold his car and gave the money to the church because he felt that is what God wanted him to do. He does not take a salary from the church because he gets a 100 percent disability pension from the government.

To explain faith, he gave the illustration of needing a full-time assistant. He asked a Liberty graduate to become his minister of music, "because I knew that the church needed the help and I could see what music would do for the church. I offered to pay $50 a week out of my own pocket, but the church offered the person $100 a week." In response to this step of faith, the offerings jumped $100 per week. Martelli testified, "We never suffered a financial need even when we took on the additional cost of a minister of music."

A year later, the church did the same thing when a youth director was needed. A Liberty graduate was added to the staff, and within a short period of time he had gathered a Bible study of approximately 60 young people on Wednesday night. Martelli noted, "We had been receiving very little in the Wednesday night offering, but because the youth director was doing such a good job, offerings on Wednesday nights jumped between $150 and $225, which took care of the needs for the additional worker."

Asked to define the gift of faith, Martelli said, "It is

the ability to motivate others to live by faith." He believes a person shares what he has been given, and those who have the gift of faith are able by their total ministry to build up faith in other believers. He goes on to say, "I have the gift of faith and, by showing what God has done in my life, I exhort other people to a life of faith." He also defined it negatively: "The gift of faith is not the gift to do the miraculous, it is not having a handle on God." By this negation, Martelli rules out the third interpretation of the gift of faith (interventional).

When asked if his faith has grown, Martelli said, "Yes, my faith has grown as I have exercised it." When asked how others can grow their faith, he answered that faith grows when several steps are taken. First, faith begins in retrospect. A person must know what God has done in his life and must see how the present fits into the past. Second, a person must become a clean vessel. One must realize that faith is letting God do things through him; the person living by faith does not do anything by himself.

In the third step, faith must take the future look. "One is never a failure if he walks in faith. The immediate result may seem like failure, but the person must take the eternal look and see things as God sees them." In the fourth place, others can motivate a person to greater faith. Martelli feels that he can help people grow in faith when they have sorrows, because God helped him overcome his problems. When he identifies those who have motivated him to more faith, he thinks of Jerry Falwell. To this he says, "I learned from Jerry Falwell to think big, and I learned to trust God. If God is in the church, God will do a big job."

A. *Faith and location.* When Martelli was asked to relate faith to location, he noted, "There is absolutely no doubt in my mind that God called me to Holden,

Massachusetts." He said most of his family was Catholic when he made a profession of faith.

They called me a fanatic and a traitor to Catholicism. Yet when I announced that I was coming to Holden to start a church, my father-in-law, who had made a profession, told me, "Pastor, when I see what God is doing in your life, it makes me want to follow you." That was not the basis of my faith; his testimony was reassurance to my faith.

B. *Faith and doctrine.* Martelli says that faith comes before doctrine. Once a person makes a profession of faith, he can grow his doctrine and, at this point, "doctrine becomes vital for Christianity." He believes a Christian cannot grow without doctrine and, in that relationship, a church cannot grow without doctrine.

C. *Faith and objectives.* Martelli believes the objective of a church is to win lost people to Jesus Christ. He has demonstrated the gift of evangelism in his personal life, and his preaching continues to be evangelistic.

Martelli believes the pastor is responsible to keep the objectives of the church in focus. "I am not a dictator, but I will lead my people, and I see that God wants us to win the lost to Christ. I will lead them in that direction."

Martelli was asked to reflect on his faith when a large group of people left the church. He responded, "What looked like failure, or a decline in church growth, could have been God's will for this church." He went on to say that he would not judge the people, for many of those had professed Christ in his church. Also, he indicated that he did not lose any of his faith. He was encouraged by remembering how Dr. Falwell announced that Thomas Road Baptist Church was facing a severe crisis when the FCC (Federal Communications Commission) was examining the church. He remembers that Falwell explained that the whole ministry could be lost. "The example of Falwell's faith in a time of crisis kept me going in my own crisis."

A group of people from his church began traveling to a charismatic Bible institute class. They returned to the church and began "forcing things," according to Martelli. "They wanted to make the church charismatic and force their teaching on us." They wanted to change the nature of the church. When he refused, they left. However, Martelli states, "The fact that people continued to make professions of faith after they left indicated to me that we are still doing what God originally called us to do, to reach Wachusett Valley for Jesus Christ."

D. *Faith and principles.* Martelli says that the principles of saturation evangelism do not work in a northern city that is predominantly Roman Catholic. He feels that the lack of Protestants in the area makes it difficult to use "every available means, to reach every available person, at every available time." By that, Martelli meant that it was difficult to use advertising to motivate people to attend church services, whether campaigns, Sunday school busing, or other promotions were used. But Martelli has motivated his people to witness constantly to their lost friends. Perhaps he is adapting saturation evangelism to the area and making it work in a different way.

When asked to explain any doubts in his life, Martelli said he did not doubt God, he only doubted his ability to do the work of God. "I question why God called me. I am not eloquent, I am not adequate to start a church. I am only willing to do his will."

His greatest step of faith, he said, was beginning the Christian school without proper facilities. Concerning his faith, Martelli indicated, "My only concern was to be sure the Christian school was scriptural. When I became convinced that the school was scriptural, I faced the next question: Was this the time to start the school?" Convinced of the timing, he stepped out on faith. The fact that the men of the church did not support him bothered Martelli, but "their lack of support did not make me doubt. The only doubts I had were in my ability, not in God's dependability."

CONCLUSION

John Martelli has integrated his view of faith into his gifts, calling, and basic approach to ministry. He believes that the gift of faith is vision or insight. When he knew God was calling him to Holden, Massachusetts, he obeyed and began planting a church. This was a step of faith to Martelli. When he says that faith has eyes that look to the past, within, and to the future, he bases his faith more on experience than on objective Christianity. Obviously, because Martelli identifies himself with Liberty, he accepts the authority of Scripture. But in answering questions relating to faith, there seems to be a high degree of integrating it with his experience.

It is obvious that God has uniquely prepared John Martelli for ministry in the Wachusett Valley. John has learned faith from Jerry Falwell and benefited from Liberty, yet he has adapted the methods to his hometown. Martelli has maturity and individuality. He has arrived at this position through much suffering and a variety of experiences. His faith is a blend of many facets, and the church has a bright future.

6
HARVEST BAPTIST CHURCH
Charleston, South Carolina
Marvin Wood, Pastor

Some think that a man cannot go home to plant and build a super-aggressive church to the glory of God. But Marvin Wood was brought up in Charleston, South Carolina, educated there at The Citadel, and returned in 1976 to plant the Harvest Baptist Church that averages over 500 in weekly attendance, with over $5,000 in weekly offerings. The church, worth approximately $750,000, is located on five acres of land, with an auditorium that seats 300 and enough Sunday school space to educate everyone. The church is in the process of doubling the educational space. According to Dr. Cecil Hodges, pastor of Bible Baptist Church, Savannah, Georgia, "The Harvest Baptist Church in Charleston is the most beautiful 'first' building of any new church I have ever seen."

On many occasions, the history of a new church has its roots in the conversion of its founder. As a young boy, Marvin Wood thought he was a Christian because he was brought up and baptized in a church. He went to The Citadel, a military college in Charleston, where he was a starter on the football team. After college, he was recommended for Sears Training School in Orlando, Florida, and there joined a Baptist church and was asked to be superintendent of the junior department. His first job was in Merritt Island, Florida, at a Sears store where he did not want to work, in a department he did not want to manage. Across the aisle at the Sears store in the vacuum cleaner and sewing machine department were several young men who were aggressive soul-winners. They met every morning for prayer. One asked Marvin, "Are you saved?" He said, "Yes," not realizing that he was lost.

One of the salesmen, Ernie Weaver, had worked nearby in the space program at Cape Canaveral and was laid off after the Apollo project was finished. He ended up working on commission selling vacuum cleaners. Ernie saw his layoff as part of God's plan for his life. Marvin Wood was amazed at Ernie's acceptance of the "demotion" in life. The two men struck up a deep friendship. Marvin said, "I must have asked him ten thousand questions about the Bible." He confessed, "Ernie had something that I had never experienced in life." Finally, one night when he could not sleep, Wood sat up in bed and prayed, "Take my life, Lord; I give it to you. I will do anything for you." Later, he looked back on that experience and realized it was his salvation. "One reason I knew was that I was immediately changed and called into the ministry." For three days he said nothing to his wife; but finally he came home one night and announced, "God has called me to preach the gospel."

Marvin Wood was attending the First Baptist Church, Merritt Island, Florida, where Dr. Adrian Rogers was then pastor. Dr. Rogers told Marvin, "Any seminary worth attending must have the full support of the pastor." Rogers recommended that Marvin Wood contact Dr. Jerry Falwell at Thomas Road Baptist Church in Lynchburg, Virginia. They had heard that Falwell was beginning a school. Wood testified, "I read the book *Church Aflame* and wanted to go to Lynchburg to learn church growth." Also he added, "I wanted to go to a school where my pastor sent me."

Wood wrote Lynchburg telling them he was a college graduate and asked, "How can I fit into the program?" The registrar wrote, "Take Bible courses for one year and then we will transfer them into the seminary program." When he arrived in Lynchburg, he found the college courses would not transfer to the seminary that would be started in the future, so he enrolled in the Bible Institute. It was his purpose to learn as much about the Bible as he could. Later, Wood testified, "God had to teach me something about faith, which is more important than just getting Bible knowledge or the tools of the ministry."

At the end of the year, a pastor from Charleston put tremendous pressure on Marvin Wood to leave school and come to work in a church in Charleston, South Carolina. As a young Christian, he had difficulty in handling the pressure, but he told the pastor no. It was a step of faith, for Wood was doing what God wanted, not what others pressured him to do.

The following year, he left the Institute and entered Liberty Baptist Seminary. It was there he said, "My greatest lessons were not academic ones, although I had to work hard and I learned much. My greatest lessons were being forced to trust God and to depend on him for everything. I was forced to trust him for money, direction, and his supply in my life." Before this the Woods had tried to have children but were unable to do so. Marvin and Carol Wood laid the matter before God in prayer and fasting. In response to the preaching of Dr. Falwell on faith, they decided to ask for four things from God: first, to have children; second, a home; third, financial support for school; and Marvin added a fourth request: "That my wife will not have to work."

They decided that if they were going to have a ministry of faith, they would have to begin in school. God began to answer when Carol got pregnant and had to leave work. (In the next three years, they had three children.) Then God provided a home for them in Lynchburg. Since Marvin had played football at The Citadel, he was given a coaching job with the fledgling football program at Liberty Baptist College. Finally, his parents helped to support him financially, which got him through seminary. He had stepped out on faith and God had honored his trust.

When he went to seminary, Wood had no idea of returning to Charleston to start a church. "School was just one step of faith at a time. Coming to Charleston and starting a church was just another step of faith, not a great step of faith, not a great threat to me because I had followed the Lord for three years in seminary."

Marvin's wife wanted him to candidate for an empty pulpit in Charleston, but he said no. Later she said, "He had faith that God would use him to build a bigger church than the one he turned down."

During his last semester at Liberty, Marvin went to the last row in the top of the balcony and saw a gentleman sitting alone writing on a tablet. "I was really just trying to be kind and help the gentleman," Wood said. There he met Dr. Towns, who asked him what he was going to do after graduation. When he replied, "Go to Charleston and start a church," the author recommended that he go first to Florence, South Carolina, and talk to Bill Monroe, the pastor of Florence Baptist Temple. The following week, Marvin Wood talked to Monroe, who gave him $500 to help get the church started. Then Monroe introduced Wood to the Tri-State Baptist Bible Fellowship, which financially supported him for $600 a month for two months.

Marvin spent his first two weeks in Charleston passing out flyers and contacting people about the new Harvest Baptist Church. Jerry Falwell provided the mailing list of people in Charleston (a practice no longer permitted). The new church was scheduled to meet in Goose Creek Elementary School. On Thursday before the first Sunday meeting, the chairman of the school board phoned to inform them that they could not use the building. At the last moment they met in the banquet room of the Holiday Inn. There were 7 in Sunday school, 26 in the morning service, and 33 that evening, August 22, 1976.

According to Wood, "That first Sunday we got acquainted and I shared with them my burden for beginning a church." He did not actually preach.

The biggest miracle in the life of the church was purchasing the present property and God's supply of the money. In January 1977, Wood looked at the present property, then owned by Georgia Pacific, who only wanted to sell him 200 frontage feet for $60,000. He turned it down, and the church prayed and searched everywhere for property. Finally, a real estate man helping the church locate property showed Wood the Georgia Pacific land again in August 1977. Wood told him, "Write up a proposal for 300 frontage feet instead of 200 feet and offer them 7 percent instead of 8½ percent, and make the total offer for $46,000 rather than $60,000." The real estate agent said, "I do not expect Georgia Pacific to sell, but I will make the offer anyway." They accepted the offer and wanted $9,000 down.

From the beginning, God has blessed the church financially. One reason is that they have given 15 percent to missions. Also, the church had been putting $200 a week aside for its building payment, long before they found property. As a result, when they got the property, they needed to raise only $15,000 in twelve weeks for the total purchase price. The church had its first stewardship campaign in September 1978, and paid cash for the new location when the first annual payment was due.

A contractor joined the church and became the general contractor for the new building. First, the church needed financing. Wood approached a former friend from Sears days, then managing the Chathos Foundation, which made humanitarian gifts. Wood asked them to loan the money for the new building at a low interest rate. The foundation wrote back and said that a loan was outside of their purpose, but they did send a $10,000 check. Finally, the church borrowed $200,000 from First Federal at 10½ percent interest. At the time, Wood exclaimed, "Lord, I never thought I would praise you for 10½ percent interest."

Jerry Falwell dedicated the new building in March 1980 on a Sunday afternoon. A crowd of over 500 gathered for the service.

ANALYSIS OF FAITH

When Marvin Wood was asked to define faith, he said, "Faith is believing God." He went on to state that living by faith was "doing what he wants me to do."

When asked how his faith grew, Wood testified that it grew first from Scripture, second from the lessons he had previously learned by faith (track record), and from soul-winners:

The men at Sears who asked me if I was a Christian; Dr. Rogers, who preached and motivated me to soul-winning; Dr. Falwell, who built a church on soul-winning; and Dr. Hughes (seminary dean), who stressed soul-winning.

Marvin Wood indicated he has not made a study of faith and was not even sure he possesses the gift of faith. He said, "I believe God will accomplish in Charleston what he sent me to do, if I will faithfully do my part." He was asked whether he practices (1) instrumental faith, (2) insightful faith, or (3) interventional faith. He answered, "All three. Faith is simply believing God can do what he promised."

A. *Faith and location.* Asked to assess his faith in relation to God's leading him to Charleston, Wood said:

I knew this was where God wanted me, so we just came. We didn't hesitate. As a matter of fact, I finished school on Friday, packed on Saturday, left Sunday morning, and got into Charleston Sunday night and started immediately working on the church. I had no job, no income. I just knew that was where God wanted us to build.

In explaining how God led him to Charleston, Wood gave the rational basis for choosing the area. "Charleston did not have the kind of church that I was saved in, or the kind of church (Thomas Road Baptist Church) where I was studying." Then Wood explained that he was doing more than making a rational choice.

Charleston was constantly on my mind. I sat in school and thought about Charleston and about the Air Force there, the colleges there, my relationship with The Citadel and football, and the medical school. I thought about having a national and international ministry through winning servicemen who would be sent around the world. I thought about medical missionaries who could go through the medical school and become missionaries. God put it upon my mind constantly. Just as Jerry was committed to his mountain (Liberty Mountain), so I was committed to my mountain (Charleston).

Beginning the church was a step of faith, but it was not fearful to Marvin Wood. "I had a track record of trusting God at Liberty and he had answered four specific requests." Yet, he admitted, his greatest step of faith and his most fearful step of faith was quitting work at Sears and going to school.

B. *Faith and doctrine.* In answer to "relate faith to doctrine," he said, "My faith is directly related to Bible knowledge." He continued, "The more I know what the Bible says on a subject, the more I preach on that matter."

I have faith in the doctrine that I understand from the Word of God. I always try to make sure it is not my own private interpretation but what I hear from other good men. When someone else (I respect) has a different interpretation, I want to study it, to understand his interpretation and why he believes like that. Then I come to the point where I decide for myself. God called me to preach. So, in the end, I answer to the Lord.

C. *Faith and objectives.* Wood pointed out that the objectives of a church are found in the Great Commission. Even though it is one objective, it has three aspects: (1) discipling people, (2) baptizing converts, and (3) teaching or maturing them. To Wood, there is no mystical aspect of faith when related to objectives. "Faith is simply obeying Jesus Christ and carrying out the Great Commission." He believes if he is faithful to this objective, God will bless the church.

D. *Faith and principles.* When Wood was asked to relate faith and principles, he testified, "All I knew was that God wanted me to knock on doors and win souls. I would have preached, whether I had a crowd or not." To him, faith is doing what God wanted him to do, and he did not know of any other way to build a church. He

7
CALVARY ROAD
BAPTIST CHURCH
Alexandria, Virginia
David Rhodenhizer, Pastor

The Calvary Road Baptist Church averaged over 1,000 in attendance during the fall of 1982, received an average offering of $8,000 per week, has facilities valued at almost three million dollars, and has an aggressive evangelistic outreach by radio, television, and visitation into the greater Washington, D.C., area. The church has a Christian school with 350 enrolled, and this year the church will receive approximately one million dollars in income.

Actually, the phenomenal strength and growth of Calvary Road Baptist Church is in part a result of the merger with New Life Baptist in June 1979. At that time, Calvary Road averaged around 150 in attendance and New Life averaged approximately 80. At the present, the church plans to construct a 1,000-seat auditorium that will cost around one million dollars.

The basis for growth at Calvary Road Baptist Church was initiated when David Rhodenhizer was called into full-time Christian service. He knew that God was calling him to preach, but he had a speech impediment that made it difficult for him even to say his name without stuttering. In junior high school he had been offered a scholarship to attend a rehabilitation program at Virginia Tech. Because it was away from home, and his family did not encourage him, he did not respond to the offer.

When he knew that God was calling him to preach, he spent time in prayer, wrestling with God. He reminded God, "How can I preach when I can't speak clearly?" He was not healed immediately, nor was he healed sensationally. He testifies that his healing "came gradually." Every time he tried to preach, God lifted more of his impediment from him. He testified, "I preached every opportunity I had, but people did not give me many opportunities." To that he adds with hindsight, "People did not try to dissuade me from preaching; it's the fact that they did not encourage me that hurt." Today, he feels people were kind to him, not wanting to hurt his feelings.

When David Rhodenhizer publicly told people that he was called to preach, he considered that announcement as "burning my bridges behind me. I knew that people would not believe me, but I had to obey God rather than man." Then, he says, "The only encouragement I received was reading the Word of God and having fellowship with him. I constantly asked God to remove my impediment." Today he looks back on two facts that caused his healing. First, he announced in faith that he was called to preach (a statement that showed confidence in God's ability to heal him). A second step of faith was when he attempted to preach without the ability (demonstrating that his desire to preach was not of the flesh).

David Rhodenhizer says that another turning point in his life of faith came at the end of his first year in college. He had completed one year at Baptist Bible College, Springfield, Missouri. He had gone there because his pastor, Dr. Jerry Falwell, who had graduated from there, encouraged him in that direction. At the end of Dave's freshman year, Dr. Falwell founded Liberty (then known as Lynchburg) Baptist College, which met in the Christian education facilities of Thomas Road Baptist Church. The college did not have fully developed programs, adequate college facilities, or a complete faculty. Now Rhodenhizer testifies, "I believe that God's perfect will for my life was attending Liberty Baptist College and capturing the pioneering spirit of faith." To David Rhodenhizer, the new college was a demonstration of faith before his eyes. He saw Dr. Falwell set a goal of having 100 students in the first year, and David Rhodenhizer was one of the 153 students in that pioneer class. He recalls, "I saw how faith overcame obstacles, motivated people to become involved in the college, and produced young people to go out and plant churches." His experience at the new college left a lasting impression on his life.

After graduation David served almost two years at Berean Baptist Church, Salem, Virginia, as youth pastor; then he moved to West Huntsville (Ala.) Bible Church, again as youth director and associate pastor.

In August 1977, he was visiting with his family in Lynchburg, Virginia. God was motivating him to plant a church. He was beginning to preach with ease, although his speech problem was still evident. He drove up Liberty Mountain (before the college buildings were there) and found a quiet mountain road. He recounted, "I knew that God wanted me to start a church, but I did not know where." He remembers telling God, "I am not coming down from this mountain until you show me where I should start a church." He bowed his head against the steering wheel of the car and prayed, but does not remember how long he prayed. Slowly God brought to his mind the Alexandria area of Virginia. The people in Lynchburg call the area (made up of several cities and suburbs) "Northern Virginia." "I decided to talk to Jerry Falwell the next day," he said.

When he walked into Dr. Falwell's office, Jerry surprised him by saying, "I would like for you to come back to Virginia and start a church either in the Tidewater or in Northern Virginia." Rhodenhizer remembers surrendering to God on the spot. Because of his conversation with his pastor, he testified, "From then on I had no doubt whatsoever that God wanted me to go to Northern Virginia and start a church."

He speaks about having no fear in taking that step of faith; in fact, he said, "I was afraid *not* to go to Northern Virginia." Even though he knew Northern Virginia was the place to start a church, he had not yet found the exact spot. He recognizes that God leads by faith as a person takes one step at a time. In following his own advice, he first resigned his position at West Huntsville Bible Church. Second, he loaded all his belongings on a rental truck and drove to the Northern Virginia area. Third, he began looking for an apartment or house to rent. He had told the Lord that he would plant the church near the place where he found a house to live. Fourth, he spent about ten days getting his family settled. He remembered the words of his pastor, Dr. Falwell, "Get your wife settled and happy so she can support you. Then go out and plant the church." Dr. Falwell had said on many occasions, "The pastor can wait two weeks to get his church started, but a woman can never wait two weeks to get her house settled." The fifth step was simply to go into the neighborhood and begin knocking on doors to solicit support for the new church. In the sixth place, Dave points out that if a person does the will of God, he will provide for the needs. Before Dave left West Huntsville, his family received a love offering large enough to live on for four weeks. Then Dr. Falwell promised a gift of $1,000 a month for the next six months. Berean Baptist Church, Salem, Virginia, also made a monthly contribution to Rhodenhizer.

Rhodenhizer says that when a person believes God is leading, he ought to pray, set goals, and then state them publicly. He set a goal of having 50 people in his first service. His new church would be called New Life Baptist Church—for the "new life" that converts to Jesus Christ would experience. He had rented the Walt Whitman Junior High School on U.S. 1 for church services. That first Sunday his wife taught the children and he taught the adults. There were 51 people there, showing that God supported his step of faith. On the first anniversary, Rhodenhizer set a goal of 200; there were 213 present.

Calvary Road Baptist Church, a church in the area, was without a pastor, and had been searching for God's man for their church. Calvary Road had been deteriorating in attendance, getting just enough money to take care of basic expenses. Its greatest need was leadership. Some people had transferred their membership from Calvary Road to New Life Baptist Church because they wanted to be in an aggressive soul-winning church. Finally, when more people from Calvary Road began coming to New Life, they got together and said, "We have buildings, property, and equipment back at the other church. This new congregation needs buildings, property, and extra help to win souls." The members of New Life who had come from Calvary Road went back and began talking to their friends. Everyone seemed agreeable to a merger.

Rhodenhizer said his next step of faith involved the merger of the two churches. He recalled,

There was a chance that the merger would be a great success, or we could lose both churches. I wanted to reach the entire area for Jesus Christ, but I could not

*find any property or a permanent location. I prayed
much about the merger because I wanted to make sure
that it was of God, and not of the flesh.*

In April 1979, David Rhodenhizer was asked to candidate at Calvary Road Baptist Church. He told the people, "God called me to begin New Life Baptist Church,
therefore if I am voted upon, we must understand that
the vote includes a call for me as the pastor and a vote
for the merger of the two churches." After he
preached, 106 out of 114 present voted to call him as
the pastor.

Rhodenhizer asked the author (Towns) to come and
speak in June 1979 to perform a "marriage ceremony"
between the two churches, which assumed the name
Calvary Road Baptist Church because it was known in
the community. At that time both churches were challenged to keep the Great Commission as their objective. To this, Rhodenhizer added, "I challenged them
to saturate the entire area with the gospel and immediately begin an aggressive soul-winning program. I
knew that as long as the church was reaching out, it
would not turn within in criticism." Before the merger,
New Life Baptist Church averaged around 80 in attendance and Calvary Road Baptist Church about 150.
God honored the step of faith and the church jumped
73 percent in attendance the next year, from 226 combined attendance, to 392.

The motto for the "marriage service" was: "Two like
spirits, one great vision." When the spirits of the two
churches came together, they had one great vision of
soul-winning.

The following year the church continued to grow,
but not as aggressively as in the previous year. In 1980
there was only 19 percent growth. Rhodenhizer realized, "We were maximizing our facilities with one
service. The auditorium was filled at every service and

I realized that when an auditorium is 80 percent filled, the church will not grow."

By faith Rhodenhizer began to plan for an early church service. "This was a great step of faith because I did not know what would happen." Before adding a second church service, Rhodenhizer had set a goal of having 1,000 in attendance in the fall of 1979, but had only 950. He explained to the congregation, "This was a psychological victory, even though we did not reach our goal." Again in the spring of 1980, they set a goal of 1,000 and missed it again. After providing space by adding the second service, they reached an attendance of 1,000 in the fall of 1981 without a special attendance campaign.

Beginning on Easter Sunday, 1982, the church began offering three services: 8:00 A.M., 9:00 A.M., and 11:00 A.M., with Sunday school at 10:00 A.M. Rhodenhizer sees the third service as a step of faith that paved the way for growth in the church. "Adding the third service was a step of faith because we did not know how people would respond. Tradition is a powerful thing, and when you tamper with tradition, it is always a step of faith." He faced the alternative: "If people don't like the extra service, they will leave the church." As a result of the three services, attendance jumped in 1982 by 44 percent, reaching an average weekly attendance of 826. On many occasions, the church has gone over 1,000 in attendance. Now Rhodenhizer looks back on the times they tried to break 1,000 and could not. "That barrier of 1,000 seems very minute to us now."

The next step of faith for David Rhodenhizer was a scheduled banquet in the last part of March 1983, with Dr. Falwell scheduled to speak. Rhodenhizer planned to raise half a million dollars in cash at that banquet. They did raise the half-million dollars, so the church can start construction on a new 1,000-seat auditorium.

FAITH IS BELIEVING THE INVISIBLE CAN BE ACCOMPLISHED

When David Rhodenhizer was asked to assess the three definitions of the gift of faith (1. instrumental, 2. insightful, and 3. interventional), he identified primarily with insight or vision. But he also included interventional. He defined faith as "the ability to see the invisible and believe that it can be accomplished." When asked if faith is the same as "possibility thinking," he said, "No. Possibility thinking is believing you can do it, but faith is knowing that God can do it through you."

To Dave Rhodenhizer, "Faith is the ability to see what God can do, and he can do what people think is impossible. Faith is first vision, but faith also includes the ability to trust God to remove the mountain barriers."

To Rhodenhizer, "Having faith in God is not only assimilating the Bible, but putting it into practice. This involves announcing goals by faith so that people know beforehand what we want to accomplish." When the goal is accomplished, people know it was done in the power of God. "By that, I mean we should put God to the test; he will do what he has promised." At this point, Rhodenhizer identifies with the interventional aspect of faith.

On the other side of the picture, Rhodenhizer realizes that there have been times when he missed his goals:

I foolishly set goals that were not God's will. When I set an attendance goal of 1,000, I did not have the organizational structure to reach the people, nor did I have the room in my sanctuary to accommodate them. What I thought was a step of faith was not a step of faith.

When analyzing his faith, he says it came by reading accounts of the heroes of the Bible and trying to do what they have done. In modern life, Rhodenhizer says that Jerry Falwell has done more to strengthen his faith than anyone else.

When asked if the gift of faith is given sovereignly or developed in relation to other gifts, he said,

The gift of faith is from God. It is life to be lived. When I exercise faith in the Word of God, and God answers, my faith grows so I have more faith to serve him better.

I do not have the skills of many of my co-laborers, and I have always struggled with the speech impediment. The main strength I have in the pastorate is my ability to trust God. Anything we have accomplished is because we have put God to the test, and he has proven himself.

A. *Faith and location.* David Rhodenhizer looks back to the time when he prayed on Liberty Mountain for God to show him if he should plant a church. The circumstances clearly indicated to Rhodenhizer that God was guiding him to Northern Virginia. He sees every goal that was accomplished as verification of God's guidance to Northern Virginia. He has accepted his location by faith. When asked if God could have used him in another location, he replied, "I have never even thought of another location."

B. *Faith and doctrine.* David Rhodenhizer says that faith is based on the Bible; and the more a person knows and applies, the more faith he will have. He makes the same application to the church; the more the church knows about God (as revealed in the Bible) and what he wants to accomplish, the more faith a church will have to step out in obedience. To Rhodenhizer, faith and doctrine cannot be separated. However, a person can know doctrine without having faith; but no one has faith without knowing the Bible.

C. *Faith and objectives.* When the two churches merged, Rhodenhizer stated,

If we lose our vision of soul-winning, we will not grow. If we place nurture or fellowship before soul-winning, the church will turn in upon itself. We would probably have disagreements. Winning the lost to Jesus Christ and evangelizing Greater Washington must be our marching orders. Soul-winning will unify us and keep the church healthy.

The church has a full program of activities for nurture and fellowship, so Rhodenhizer is obviously using them in their place. He has a clear objective for the church and is able to carry out his vision.

D. *Faith and principles.* The church is committed to saturation evangelism. It has advertised on television, radio, newspapers, through flyers, and in various other ways. The church has an aggressive evangelistic program and has attendance campaigns.

Rhodenhizer applies all three aspects of faith. First, the principles of ministry and their application must be in harmony with the principles of the Word of God(instrumental); second, a leader must have a vision or burden from God on what can be accomplished (insightful); third, the leader must then launch out in faith by taking a risk. He must publicly set goals and publicly lead his congregation to trust God for big answers to prayer (instrumental).

CONCLUSION

David Rhodenhizer believes faith has all three aspects (instrumental, insightful, interventional). He has a historic basis for knowing God has called him to the ministry—his healing. He seems to be measured in stating faith goals, and is quick to admit some goals were wrongly set. The accomplishment of his goals has given him credibility in the eyes of his congregation. Now they are willing to follow his leadership when he announces greater goals for the future.

Rhodenhizer seems to have a good blend of evangelism and nurture; this is predictive of future growth. Also, he has a good blend of leadership and lay involvement, another indication of future growth. The church is planning a large auditorium and more parking, all with a view of growth. David Rhodenhizer is young, and if he can keep his present balance, the church should continue to grow.

8

FREEPORT BAPTIST CHURCH
Freeport, Illinois
Kurt Strong, Pastor

Kurt Strong graduated from Liberty Baptist Seminary and returned to Freeport, Illinois, in June 1978, to begin a church in his hometown. The church met in four different temporary locations for two years, then purchased three acres of land on a major highway and built facilities valued at $275,000. Attendance averages 135 at the morning services; the church has an annual income of $97,235. There seems to be no miraculous intervention of God to a threatening crisis and no outstanding answer to prayer that explains the growth of Freeport Baptist Church. Rather, the growth is the result of a man who faithfully ministered the Scriptures. Then God blessed the church with growth.

HISTORY OF THE CHURCH

Kurt Strong was saved as a child and grew up in the church, attending Sunday school, youth activities, and normal church pursuits. After graduating from Northern Illinois University with a degree in business management, he worked as a manager-in-training for a

Rockford firm. He got involved in the First Baptist Church of Freeport in church bus ministry, and led the high school evangelistic visitation. God began speaking to him about full-time ministry. Then, because of a 1974 recession, he lost his job; the only employment he could find was as janitor of First Baptist Church. According to Strong,

God had humbled me. After college, I had planned to be president of a corporation. I did not mind hard work and I refused to go on welfare. We had a baby coming, and I did not want to go further in debt.

During this time, God began to speak to him about the ministry. He surrendered to become a full-time bus minister, willing to go to any church that would call him. But in his heart he knew that he had not done enough. Finally, he surrendered to the call to be a pastor, and felt satisfied that he was in the will of God.

He wrote to many seminaries and decided to attend the one that had the most emphasis on evangelism in its catalog. He chose Liberty Baptist Seminary, Lynchburg, Virginia.

During his first semester at seminary, the Thomas Road Baptist Church and Liberty Baptist Seminary sponsored a conference for youth workers. During one of the general sessions, Kurt Strong felt God was telling him to return to his hometown to plant a church. This was a difficult move for him to consider. His home church, the First Baptist Church, had an effective ministry, and he did not want to be in competition with his friends. There were other, smaller evangelical churches in the community, but Kurt Strong wanted to plant a church with strong emphasis on separation and soul-winning, yet emphasizing love among its members. Since he had finished seminary in two and a half years, attending two summer schools, he graduated in 1978, then returned immediately to Freeport.

To begin the church, he visited 1,850 homes within the first two weeks of his return to Freeport. The first service was held on June 4, 1978, with 43 people present. As Kurt Strong looked out over that first week's congregation, he was greatly disappointed. After his visitation, more than 100 families had promised to attend; but not one of those families came.

The next week only 19 people returned. "I wanted to back out of my commitment, but there was no honorable way to do it. The greatest step of faith I have ever taken was to come back to the church on the third week." During that summer, Kurt Strong continued to minister. Whereas some may feel that their church went forward with a great answer to prayer, or after receiving a big gift, Kurt Strong said the church grew because he did not give up. This statement reveals his attitude toward faith, for he said to continue the church weekly was the greatest step of faith he had ever taken.

The church began meeting in an old Farm Bureau building. Next, they moved to an abandoned Evangelical United Brethren Church which had been turned into the public health center; then they went to the YMCA; and, finally, to a public school. To Kurt Strong, faith was not the miraculous supply of a new building, but continuing in whatever facilities God provided.

As soon as the church was organized, they began putting money into a building fund account. This later became the basis of growth.

Dr. Frank Schmitt, professor of Christian Education at Liberty Baptist Seminary, came for the chartering service in October 1978. As he surveyed the town with Kurt Strong, Schmitt told him they needed ten acres of ground on Pearl City Road, one of the main arteries that was just starting to be built up. Strong felt that was impossible, for the owners were asking $20,000 an acre. He confessed, "I did not have faith to believe God could give us $200,000."

As the church moved from one building to another, they prayed and continued looking for property. Everything in the city seemed closed. Two years later, Kurt Strong went back to Pearl City Road and prayed over the property. When he called the owners, they said, "Please meet us." They cut in half the price per acre. Apparently, they had tax problems and were now anxious to sell. Kurt Strong agreed to buy three acres of ground for $30,000, with an option to purchase seven more acres in five years at $10,000 per acre. The church was able to pay cash for the property. A loan for $130,000 was arranged and the church built on this property, dedicating the new building in March 1981.

FAITH IS SEEING AND UNDERSTANDING WHAT GOD IS DOING

When Kurt Strong was asked to define faith, he said, "I used to believe that faith was simply believing God to do something that is impossible." He went on to explain that a daughter was born to them in 1979 without a brain; she had only a brainstem. That meant she was capable only of involuntary motions, and sometimes for thirty-six hours she would have seizures characterized by loud screaming and involuntary shaking. On several occasions, Kurt and his wife asked God to give them faith that she would be healed. On many occasions when their daughter went into a seizure, they would claim 1 Corinthians 10:13, "There hath no temptation taken you but such as is common to man: but God is faithful, who will not suffer you to be tempted above that ye are able; but will with the temptation also make a way to escape, that ye may be able to bear it." When the pressure seemed unbearable, they claimed this verse, and within a half hour the seizures would pass. The little girl lived for eight months, but the experience left an indelible impact upon Kurt Strong.

Now he says, "Faith is the ability to see and understand what God is doing, then trusting him through every circumstance of life." To this he testified,

I did not have faith that she would be healed, but through the whole experience, I had faith to see God's plan in my life and totally trust God with my daughter. Now I can trust God for every situation because I know he is working in me and in the church.

When Kurt Strong was asked to define the gift of faith, he said, "It is the ability to see something that seems impossible to accomplish, then trusting God to accomplish it." When asked if he had the gift of faith, Kurt Strong replied, "Periodically I think I have experienced the gift of faith, but I have not maintained it on a consistent basis throughout my ministry."

When viewing the gift of faith as (1) instrumental, (2) insightful, and (3) interventional, Kurt Strong seems to say that the faith that he has experienced is not the last type, which is interventional faith. But at the same time he is saying that faith is the first two aspects. Faith is an instrument in the work of God and faith is insight that sees what God is doing or can do.

Kurt Strong responded that his faith has grown since he started the church. When asked how his faith has grown, he answered with four points.

"First, my faith grows when I have the security of knowing that God is using me." He points to a recent change in his thinking concerning church leadership. Several people told him that he needed more organization to get more done in the church. A neighboring pastor helped him organize the people into five commissions within the church. Now the laymen are involved in church leadership, and he sees them growing in spiritual nurture through involvement. "I am encouraged when I realize I am not standing alone, but I am standing with my people."

Therefore, to Kurt Strong, his ability to organize is an important step in the growth of his church. "By faith, I have learned organization which has helped my ministry." He indicated that previous to this, "faith was only a vision, but I could not accomplish my vision." He responded, "If faith is the substance of things hoped for (Heb. 11:1), I was not getting what I wanted. Now I have substance in my ministry because I have more than a dream. I have organization in my church that makes reaching my community a reality."

Kurt Strong indicated that a second way his faith has grown is by learning to challenge or confront people with the Word of God. "I was too reluctant when I first began my ministry." He said that, in the spirit of Matthew 18:15, he has gone to his people in love with the truth. This is another way of saying that he is more honest with people. Also, he has challenged other people not to gossip, but to be honest with each other. By adding honesty to lay involvement, "Our people are more responsible to the church; hence they are more involved and they are growing by faith." Kurt Strong points out that in the past year there have been fewer people who left the church than in former years. As a result, the church is stronger. He stated, "Because we have a stronger church, I have stronger faith in God."

The third step that grew his faith involved going through trials. Because of the birth defect of their daughter, Kurt said, "I now can trust God for everything in my life; because of trials, my faith is stronger."

Kurt Strong said that the last thing to grow his faith was his relationship with men of faith. He mentioned Jerry Falwell, stating, "I marveled at his faith and learned from his ability to trust God." The second person who meant the most to him was Bill Gothard, who taught him to live by biblical principles.

A. *Faith and location.* It was a step of faith to return to Freeport to plant a church. Kurt Strong was embarrassed by his former life (even though he was a Christian) and wondered if the people would respond to him as a pastor. Also, he did not want to conflict with the ministry of First Baptist Church because he had rededicated his life there and had been active in its ministry. Yet, when God called him to return to Freeport, he realized, "It was not a matter of what the people thought, but what was the will of God. When I realized that God was giving me a burden for Freeport, I realized I could not go anywhere else." When asked what would have happened if he had gone to another location, he responded, "God could have used me at another location, but not as greatly. By going elsewhere, I would have said no concerning Freeport; I would have had a limited future elsewhere."

B. *Faith and doctrine.* Kurt Strong is deeply committed to the precepts of Christianity. He accepts them as the Word of God because of the claims of Scripture, but also because they work in his life and through his ministry at the church. It is not a question of whether God could have blessed him if he believed otherwise; he would not have done otherwise. The foundation for church growth in doctrine and faith is basing vision upon the pure Word of God.

C. *Faith and objectives.* When asked about his objectives, Strong answered, "I have not changed my vision since I left Liberty. I still desire to win people to Christ. By faith, God shares his vision with me and I obey his objectives, his Word, and his principles to accomplish it."

D. *Faith and principles.* When asked about the principles of super-aggressive evangelism, he indicated,

"Faith is vision to see what God wants to accomplish, then doing it." By faith, Strong believes he must aggressively obey the principles of the Word of God to accomplish the work of God. Even though soul-winning is his primary thought, he has spent more time pastoring his people than in door-to-door evangelism. When viewing the conditions of Freeport, he sees the necessity of building a strong congregation that will nurture the people. From that foundation he will reach out with evangelism.

When he came to Freeport, Strong mentioned that his greatest doubt was over money. "I had questions concerning whether we would get enough money to accomplish our vision." Yet after five years he explains, "I do not now have the doubts about money that I had. I believe God will provide for our needs, because I have seen what he has done over the years."

CONCLUSION

Kurt Strong views faith and vision (insight) and uses the Word of God to carry out his vision for the church (instrument). His articulated view of faith has changed since leaving Lynchburg. Whereas he once believed faith was interventional, he does not now hold that view. The growth of the church seems to reflect his attitude toward faith. He sees what God is doing and works to accomplish it. Kurt Strong seems to have an objective-based Christianity that is reflected by the measured growth of the church.

9

NEW LIFE
BAPTIST CHURCH
New Cumberland, Pennsylvania
Ronnie Riggins, Pastor

Ronnie Riggins describes himself as meek and reluctant. He says he would probably never have planted the church except that a layman who owned an empty church building invited him to come and begin an aggressive soul-winning church in New Cumberland, Pennsylvania, a suburb of Harrisburg. Within three months, there was a disagreement with the owner of the building over church polity, and the infant church moved into a fire hall, then into a public school. The church continued its steady growth, and four years later bought acreage on I-83 and constructed a $300,000 building with an auditorium that would seat 300 people. The attendance has decreased 15 percent in the past year due to a deemphasis in the bus ministry; but the financial offerings, drive-in attendance, and other areas of the church continue to grow.

Ronnie Riggins was a member of the original freshman class at Liberty Baptist College. He knew very little about the college, not even its rules or objectives. He knew only that his pastor had recommended Liberty to him. He spent his time at the school in evangelism, working with Jim Vineyard, then director of Sunday school busing at Thomas Road Baptist Church.

He graduated in May 1975, and became director of Sunday school busing at the Shenandoah Valley Baptist Church, Winchester, Virginia. He testified, "I always had a burden to start a church. Since Jerry Falwell had emphasized Virginia, I thought I would plant a church somewhere in Virginia."

While working at Shenandoah Valley Baptist Church, he took his day off to travel to towns in different areas of Virginia to survey them with the possibility of starting a church. After surveying several towns, he found no open doors and confessed, "I became frustrated and discouraged." One day while returning home from Alexandria, Virginia, he pulled his car over to the side of the road and told God, "I'm not going to force the issue of starting a church anymore. I'd like to start a church, but I will be faithful in my bus ministry at Shenandoah Valley Baptist Church." In essence, Ronnie Riggins surrendered his future to God. He left the matter with the Lord and put his energies into the bus ministry.

Three months later, a Christian businessman from New Cumberland, Pennsylvania, heard Dr. Jack Hyles, Pastor, First Baptist Church, Hammond, Indiana, speak in Harrisburg, Pennsylvania. The businessman determined that an aggressive soul-winning church was needed in the New Cumberland area; and since he owned a church building, he wrote to Jack Hyles to ask for a recommendation of a young man to come start a church. Rev. Jim Vineyard had moved to the First Baptist Church from Lynchburg. He received the letter and recommended Ronnie Riggins to the businessman. Within two weeks, Ronnie Riggins traveled to New Cumberland to survey the area. Riggins determined that a church could be built in the suburbs of South Harrisburg.

Ronnie Riggins moved to New Cumberland in November 1975, spent two weeks visiting in the area, and held the first service on December 7, 1975. There were 21 people in Sunday school and 45 in church. An offering of $246 was received.

Within forty-five days, attendance was averaging over 100. Riggins indicated that the crowd came because: (1) over 5,000 brochures were mailed to everyone in the area; and (2) Dr. Falwell sent a letter to everyone on his mailing list encouraging them to attend the new church (a policy Falwell no longer practices).

Riggins testifies that the timing for the new church accounted for its growth. Many people in mainline denominational churches watched Jerry Falwell on television and considered him their pastor. Some, but not all of them, came to the new church from the beginning. Therefore, there were few financial problems in getting the church started.

Within three months, a disagreement arose between the owner of the church building and Ronnie Riggins over authority and leadership in the church. Riggins felt that he had to give spiritual leadership to the congregation, yet the businessman (because he owned the building) felt he could give directions to the church. Riggins testifies,

The biggest step of faith I ever took in my life was to move out of the church building into the fire hall. I was only twenty-four years old and just getting started. The church was only four months old. The church building had stained-glass windows, pews, and an amplification system. It had all we needed for our ministry.

Some people warned Riggins, "You will lose all of your financial support and regular members. You will have only a few children left." After several long periods of prayer, Riggins was convinced that he was doing the will of God. He did not know who would follow him into the fire hall. When the move was made, almost everyone in the church followed him. What the owner of the building did not realize was that the people were committed neither to a building nor to someone's financial support. They were committed to a church with objectives similar to the ministry they received from Dr. Falwell on television. They did not realize they would be in temporary facilities for one month and a school building for three and a half years.

The church continued to grow monthly while they were in the public school. During the next three years, they had accumulated almost $25,000 in the building fund. Finally, they found acreage on I-83 and sold $200,000 in bonds to finance the new facilities. The church also had to borrow $75,000 from the bank to get into the building. The new facilities were occupied in 1979 and attendance increased 30 percent the next year.

FAITH IS TAKING GOD AT HIS WORD

When asked to define faith, Riggins said, "Faith is just taking God at his word, without question, and obeying him." When his faith is compared to the terms (1) instrumental, (2) insightful, and (3) interventional, he seems to say that faith is an instrument to be used in the ministry of the Lord. Yet when Riggins was asked to define the gift of faith, he said, "It is the ability to believe God for the impossible." He noted that the Bible called the gift of faith "the measure of faith." He defined the word *measure* to mean "the size of faith." Asked if he has the gift of faith, Ronnie said, "I do not know if I have the gift of faith, but I do know that I have faith, and that my faith is stronger now than when I began the church."

Riggins was asked how his faith has grown.

First, by study of the Word of God and applying its principles to my life. Second, I have grown by my times of prayer and getting answers from God. In the third place, faith grows by exercise. When I use what I have, my faith grows to trust God for bigger things. In the fourth place, my faith has developed by being around godly men who have faith. Jerry Falwell has done more than anyone else to strengthen my faith and to challenge me to trust God for big things. The fifth step is simply to be faithful.

Once Riggins asked Dr. William Pennell, pastor of Forrest Hills Baptist Church, Decatur, Georgia, "What do I need as a young man?" Pennell answered him, "Walk with God." To this, Riggins says that as he grows in his total experience as a Christian, he will grow in faith. Riggins adds a sixth step to growing faith. "Faith grows through trials." To prove this point, Riggins quotes, "that the trying of your faith worketh patience" (James 1:3). "Trials work to purify the Christian and draw him nearer to Jesus Christ. This process causes the person to grow in Christ."

Finally, Riggins indicated that a person grows in faith by being contented in the Lord. He indicated that, "On occasions we did not know how God would put food on the table, but he has always answered our prayers. When we trust God, we must be absolutely satisfied with the results God gives, or we are not trusting him." Riggins testified that he as pastor seemed always to be under financial pressure, but God taught him how to live by faith on a day-to-day basis.

A. *Faith and location.* Riggins said that he knows God led him to New Cumberland. When seeking the will of God, he used the "open door" principle. "I tried to find a place to start a church but could not. When God opened the door with an invitation, I knew that was where I should go." When asked if he had any doubts about going to New Cumberland, especially in view of losing the building after three months, Riggins answered, "My faith about the city has never been shaken. New Cumberland is the place God wanted me to be."

B. *Faith and doctrine.* Riggins feels that the Bible and doctrine are the foundation of faith. He says his faith is based on Scripture, and during the interview, he frequently quoted Scripture to illustrate the basis for his faith.

When asked about the credibility of doctrine, Riggins has no doubts about what he believes. In reply to questions about doubts, he said that, since his faith is Bible based, he does not question God; nor does he have doubts when the expressions of his faith are based on the Word of God. He notes, "Faith is not measured by my sincerity but by its source, the Bible."

C. *Faith and objectives.* To Riggins, the purpose of the church is soul-winning. He has not changed this objective, but recently he has balanced it with a stronger emphasis on teaching or nurturing his members.

When he was asked about changing his objectives, he responded, "Why should I change? The Great Commission is still the purpose of the church. I am still committed to winning soul, but now I will emphasize building up people in the Word of God."

D. *Faith and principles.* Riggins said that super-aggressive principles have worked to some extent, but he has found that Pennsylvania is different from the South, and has its own need for specific methods.

CONCLUSION

Even though Riggins says he is a reluctant leader, he has given mature leadership to New Life Baptist Church. His view of faith seems to reflect his personality and his community context. When he says, "Faith is believing God for the impossible," he does not mean that God will produce New Testament signs, nor that God will do the empirical miracle in the life of his church. To Riggins, faith is insight or vision, seeing the "impossible." Then he works to accomplish the "apparent impossibility," rather than waiting for a crisis to be solved by luck or circumstances.

Of all the Liberty graduates, Riggins seems to have the most objective or traditional approach to faith. It is grounded in Scripture. What has been accomplished by faith is simply the application of the Word of God to the situation in which Ronnie Riggins finds himself.

10
FREDERICKTOWNE BAPTIST CHURCH
Frederick, Maryland
Gary Byers, Pastor

Gary Byers, a young pastor, seems to have gone the cycle in church ministry from the eager youth evangelist to a Bible-teaching pastor. He entered Lynchburg (now Liberty) Baptist College in the first year of the institution, traveled with an evangelistic singing group, and was introduced on the nationwide telecast of the Old-Time Gospel Hour by Jerry Falwell as a super-aggressive "preacher boy." He traveled with Dr. Falwell as a friend.

Dr. Falwell inaugurated an evangelistic crusade in Frederick which ultimately led to the founding of the church; but it has had a rocky path of growth. In four out of eight years, the church has registered minus or no growth.

The church began with a super-aggressive vision of reaching the entire Frederick area. Yet, in the past few years, it has evolved from an attempt at being a metropolitan-type church into a neighborhood-type church, and in the latter role has had its best growth because of its well-rounded ministry. Byers has also evolved from an evangelistic preacher to an expository preacher.

Gary Byers graduated from Liberty Baptist College in 1974 when he was only twenty-two years of age. During his senior year, he had been traveling on weekends to Shenandoah Valley Baptist Church in Winchester, Virginia, approximately 180 miles away from Lynchburg. He visited on the bus routes, worked with the young people, and taught Sunday school. The training was invaluable and he enjoyed the evangelistic ministry. Halfway through his senior year, Byers and three other young people from Liberty (who worked with him at Shenandoah Valley) were invited to participate in an evangelistic crusade designed to begin a church in Frederick, Maryland, some fifty miles from Winchester. The crusade was the plan of an active member at Shenandoah Valley.

In January 1974, Jerry Falwell held a rally in Frederick, Maryland, with approximately 250 people in attendance. After this initial meeting, the pastor of Shenandoah Valley continued weekend evangelistic meetings for the next month. During those next four weeks, Byers traveled from Lynchburg to Winchester on Friday afternoons, then on to Frederick for Friday and Saturday night meetings. Attendance began dwindling in the meetings and they moved from the rented Church of the Brethren building to the Salvation Army Citadel in the inner city. Attendance reached a low of approximately 25 people, but in the midst of rather disappointing results, Byers felt direction from God to stay and start a church.

Finally, on Palm Sunday 1974, the church held its first service in an elementary school with 32 people present. The group was composed of a number of students from Liberty Baptist College and Byers' family and friends from his hometown about sixty miles away in the Washington, D.C., area. The nucleus of the new church was two local families. To advertise the new church, an ad announced: "Jerry Falwell says, 'A new church is starting in Frederick soon. Watch this space for name and place.' " Two weeks later, the same ad stated, "Jerry Falwell says, 'Fredericktowne Baptist Church is glad to be in Frederick,' " and the time and place were given.

After graduation in May, Gary Byers moved into a motel in Frederick and began his ministry. He was out walking and praying near the motel and saw an empty house. Byers claimed it for the Lord. Finding the owner, the church offered to rent it. The owner asked, "How did you know we were getting ready to put it on the market?" They did rent it, and the home became the center for church activity. Gary Byers lived there, along with the men who were assisting him. During that first year, the church grew by 116 percent, from 60 to 130, but it was a very unstable group, overloaded with children. The aggressive evangelism of the students, plus the Sunday school bus route, accounted for the growth. The church was meeting in a school building (the old home was the headquarters).

FAITH IS VISUALIZING WHAT GOD INTENDS TO DO

When Byers was asked which of the three concepts of faith expressed his view (1. instrumental, 2. insightful, and 3. interventional), he indicated that faith is insight and/or vision. His definition of faith is one he has adopted from others: "Faith is visualizing what God intends to do in a given situation and then acting in harmony with God's plan." His concept of the gift of faith is consistent with his definition of faith. "A person who has the gift of faith has the special ability to see a great thing that God wants to do and then to make the right decisions that will bring it to pass."

A. *Faith and location.* Gary Byers is sure that God led him to Frederick. "I never had a serious doubt about the location." While he was in college, his mother had sent him a clipping from the *Washington Post* concerning the death of the football coach at Liberty. On the back of the clipping was a map showing three places in the Baltimore-Washington, D.C., area. Frederick, Maryland, was one of three cities that appeared on the map. He never even studied the map until after the pastor of Shenandoah Valley asked Byers if he would like to help in the crusade at Frederick, which might lead to starting a church. Later, when he noticed the map on the back of the clipping, he was astounded to see Frederick, Maryland. He never remembered hearing about that city before, and now it was popping up again before him. He said about the situation, "Although I never have considered myself much of a mystic, this time I really did have a sense that God wanted me there; so I told them I would help in the crusade."

As Gary Byers began praying about Frederick, he used the "closed door" concept of faith, rather than the "open door." By that he prayed, "God, I believe you have opened the doors for me to go to Frederick, and I'm going. If you don't want me there, you will have to close the door."

At the time, Byers made a list of reasons why he felt God wanted him in Frederick. To him it was an impressive argument. These things involved a building, key families to start the work, students from Liberty to help, and especially agreement among those involved in the crusade that he should stay. He prayed on several occasions, "Stop me if you do not want me there." Today he reasons that, since God did not close the door, he found the right location by faith. Even in the most difficult times his sense of calling was not shaken. He had that same confidence in moving to the empty house as headquarters, and the school building for Sunday services at first, and the facilities of the local Seventh Day Adventist church later. On that same basis the church purchased their present property. He sees a correct decision to operate by faith as resulting in a supernatural peace "that passeth all understanding." Throughout all these decisions he felt he has had such direction from God for his ministry.

B. *Faith and doctrine.* According to Byers, "Right thinking produces the blessing of God. The blessing of God should result in church growth. And right thinking comes from correct doctrine." While not adhering to any specific denominational or associational doctrinal statement, Byers holds to traditional Baptistic beliefs. When he hears about other church growth, especially when built on doctrine different from his, he states, "Assuming that church growth is evidence of the blessing of God, I don't really understand why God blesses different churches, some of which have different doctrine.

"It seems to me," he stated, "that God deals with everybody in a different way. I just can't imagine myself doing some of the things I see others doing, and still experiencing the blessing of God on my ministry." In the area of faith and doctrine, Byers sees God working in the hearts of all people who agree on major church doctrine. In the area of church growth and doctrine he said, "It appears to me that God blesses a person for what he has that is right (correct doctrine) and doesn't necessarily penalize him for what is not right."

In applying faith to his doctrine, Byers looks back and can see a definite correlation between his graduate studies and his understanding of doctrine. "The more I learned," he said, "the better I was able to crystallize my doctrine. That made me feel much more sure of myself and authoritative in my ministry to others. The whole process gave great impetus to my faith."

When Byers first started the church, doctrine was extremely important to him. Over the years he has not changed his doctrine, but his priority on content is not the same. He states, "My practical application has sharpened, but my doctrine has not changed. I feel that as the pastor, if I am on the cutting edge of life, God will bless me. Also, I need to apply doctrine to life as a father and husband and in my personal walk before God." Byers states, "If I believe right and if I live right, God will be at work in my life and ultimately that should produce church growth in my ministry."

When viewing doctrine, Byers says, "Simply knowing correct truths of Christianity does not build a church. Doctrine must be supernaturally dynamic so that it changes daily life. When this happens, the life-changing influence of Christians attracts others to Christ, and church growth will be a natural result." In addition to applying doctrine to his personal life, Gary Byers said, "Interpersonal relationships are imperative for church growth." He noted that some people believe the cardinal truths of Christianity, but they cannot get along with anyone else. This deters church growth. "If a church correctly teaches and applies doctrine, people will love one another and the church will grow." But he adds, "I suppose the variable in the whole equation to me is, 'Does church growth necessarily indicate the blessing of God?' History has taught that an institution can grow large without both correct doctrine and the blessing of God. In the final analysis, correct doctrine and that rather nebulous 'blessing of God' are far more important to me than church growth."

C. *Faith and objectives.* Byers states plainly, "My objective is to make F.B.C. the best church that F.B.C. can be—to reach the full potential that God has for our church, regardless of what others project either for us or for themselves." Going through the original years at Liberty, Byers faced the pressure of living up to the expectation of the faculty and other students. He was called a "preacher boy," and many of the ministerial students felt they had to do as well as Jerry Falwell. When viewing this standard, Byers said, "I failed miserably." He went on to say, "I got so concerned about numbers, and when they didn't come I felt a total failure."

Byers took a decided turn in his ministry when he moved into the SDA building. At the time he had three deacons, and two opposed the move. But, according to him, Fredericktowne Baptist Church had no alternative. All three deacons quit. One of the deacons did not resign in protest. He was a graduate of Liberty Home Bible Institute and had begun to serve as interim pastor in a small country church. He later started a church in Gettysburg, Pennsylvania, and Byers collected money and has helped him from the beginning. The other two deacons quit and joined another church in the area.

Byers said, "When we went into the SDA building, I quit trying to reach other people's standards for me. I knew I couldn't make it, so I just tried to do the best I was capable of doing and forgot about what others did or thought." It was more than an internal change in the pastor; there was also a change in his ministerial philosophy. He had seen a number of people make professions of faith, but they did not follow through on their professions. He decided to spend more time preaching to his people and discipling individuals. He shifted his pulpit ministry from evangelism to nurture. He called it "pastoring the people from the pulpit."

"When I went into the SDA building, I felt like a failure." Byers described the change, "I knew I was as committed to the Lord as I knew how to be, so I just had to hold on and see what he was going to do. That decision freed me up to be a better pastor."

There was another major change when Byers entered the SDA building. His church philosophy had gradually become more legalistic than it had been upon graduation from LBC. This legalism was a natural outgrowth of his following the methodology and attitudes of other pastors in his quest to build a large church. But these were convictions that Byers himself did not feel comfortable with. "I did not feel free to take a stand for what I really believed in. After those deacons and other families of similar convictions left, I had freedom to preach what I thought God was telling me without fear of mutiny."

Finally, Byers testified that in moving to the SDA building, he moved away from super-aggressive evangelism. He had known how to go door to door and witness and he had also known how to get children to ride his bus to church. But he did confess, "I did not know how to build a super-aggressive church, and I really did not know where I was going with the super-aggressive church."

Byers indicated he had the privilege of "starting over twice." After the first split came over the property in 1977, and ended with the associate pastor starting a new church in 1978, he still wasn't sure where he was going. When the deacons left in 1980, he changed to a nurturing model. He was in his last semester of seminary by this time and felt that he knew where he wanted to go. When asked the purpose of the church, he stated, "I still believe the purpose of the church is to make disciples of all nations, to baptize them and to teach them all things." But he now defines the word *discipling* differently: "Evangelism means more than getting persons to make decisions; it includes follow-up." He still believes that the purpose of the church is evangelism, but he applies evangelism in a broader sense.

D. *Faith and principles.* Byers admits, "I started out trying to be super-aggressive, but I found that I could not do it right, and I did not know where I was going with it." He testified that, as he went door to door, "many of my decisions were not lasting. I would get people to make decisions at the front door, but I could not get them to the church. Some who did come to church would not come forward and make a public profession. Of these who did come forward, most lasted only a few months." Upon the move into the SDA church, he felt free to change his principles. Byers began attending Liberty Seminary in 1978, and he took courses in Bible, administration, education, and counseling. He wanted to apply these principles to see if they would work. He began to see counseling as a greater avenue to minister to the needs of people. "If these folks can get straightened out," he reasoned, "then they will reach others." He feels that this has proven true. In 1982 he found that he was able to lead more people to Christ who stayed in the church through counseling than he had personally reached in door-to-door evangelism in previous years.

Byers testified, "I was presenting the gospel to fewer people, but was getting more results and the church was growing." He has gotten into family, marital, premarital, drug, alcohol, and crisis counseling. "When my church and I saw the positive result of my counseling, it increased all our faith," he said. "It also made me a more authoritative leader. People really felt I could help them find answers to their problems."

With this change came a new emphasis in his pulpit ministry. The people supported Byers, and he became known as an expositor of the Word. With this change he gave more attention to study. After graduation from Liberty Baptist Seminary (1980), he enrolled in Baltimore (Md.) Hebrew College. With his change from evangelistic preaching to expositional preaching, the people began bringing their friends and relatives, leading to church growth. Technically speaking, the church went from front door evangelism to side door evangelism, accounting for the growth in 1981–82.

CONCLUSION

Gary Byers began his ministry with Jerry Falwell as an example and standard. Probably his concept of faith was interventional. Yet he could not produce the numerical growth expected of him. When viewing the history of Fredericktowne Baptist Church, there seems to be no great answer from God in which Byers stepped out on faith. Obviously there were crises, but no supernatural interventions by faith. If his view of faith was interventional, he was not able to make it work in his ministry.

After two major crises, Byers made a philosophical change in his ministry. He did not repudiate his relationship to Dr. Falwell, but intensified his ties to Liberty. The change involved Byers' bringing his concept of faith into line with his personal application of Christianity and his experience in Frederick. He now interprets faith as insight or vision of what God expects of him. Also, the change involved Byers' adapting his style of ministry to his own life-style and to the new community contextual factors in which he found himself. As a result of his change, Byers seems to minister from inner strength, because he is using his gifts rather than imitating someone else.

Byers still claims that Falwell taught him more faith than any other person. However, it seems evident that even though one credits the other, today Falwell and Byers express their faith differently.

11
BALTIMORE COUNTY
BAPTIST CHURCH
Reistertown, Maryland
Bob Gehman, Pastor

Bob Gehman was born into a Mennonite home in Lancaster County, Pennsylvania, where he was taught the Scriptures and attended church. His conversion was not spectacular. He said, "The average Mennonite family attempts to win its children to Jesus Christ. When I was thirteen, my mother had me pray to receive Christ."

At seventeen, Bob Gehman moved to Philadelphia to attend barber school. When the Vietnam war came, he was faced with the prospect of being drafted. Being a Mennonite pacifist, he moved to Washington, D.C., to fulfill his military requirement serving in a hospital. It was there he met Dr. Herb Fitzpatrick, pastor of Riverdale Baptist Church who was visiting one of his parishoners after surgery. Fitzpatrick invited Gehman to church. At first young Gehman resisted because it was not a Mennonite fellowship. Because of Fitzpatrick's persistence, Gehman attended, liked it, and became involved in the singles' ministry class taught by Lois Fitzpatrick, the pastor's wife. The class consisted of more than a hundred young people living away from their parents in metropolitan Washington, D.C.

Gehman grew in the Lord as he led singles to Jesus Christ and studied doctrine in Bible study groups. It was there he realized that God was speaking to his heart concerning full-time Christian service. At first Gehman considered Baptist Bible College in Springfield, Missouri.

"My call to the ministry was not a crisis experience, but gradually God spoke to me about serving him full time." Like the gradual dawning of a day, Gehman came to the conclusion that he should become a pastor of a church, like the one Dr. Herb Fitzpatrick was building. One Sunday after the evening fellowship, he stood to commit his life to full-time Christian service. When he got home at approximately 1:00 A.M., Gehman phoned his parents to tell them of his decision. They were very supportive, his mother remarking, "We felt all along that you would be a preacher, and we have been praying to that end."

The authors, Jerry Falwell and Elmer Towns, visited Riverdale Baptist Church recruiting students for Liberty Baptist College, which they were starting in the fall of 1971. Gehman had already made application to Baptist Bible College. Pastor Fitzpatrick said, "I don't see any reason why this college will not succeed; you ought to pray about going there." Gehman put in his application. He then learned that all freshmen would be given a free trip to Israel if (1) they were passing, (2) had their bill paid, and (3) did not have discipline problems. This confirmed his decision inasmuch as he had been praying God to allow him to go to the Holy Land.

When he arrived at Liberty, Gehman lived in a large two-story frame home with twenty-three other boys, all of them sharing one bathroom with one bathtub. Classes were meeting in Sunday school rooms of the church. The college used the church gym, a church dining hall, a church office, and church advertising facilities.

Gehman indicated, "I was part of a pioneering college that gave me the pioneering spirit to go out and pioneer a church." He went on to say, "From the first year at Liberty, I've never had anything else in my mind but to go start a church. I've been single-minded in my vision."

Dr. Fitzpatrick had families driving more than fifty miles from Baltimore, Maryland, to attend his church in greater Washington, D.C. Fitzpatrick suggested to Bob Gehman that he go to Baltimore and plant a new church. A college student, George Can, volunteered to visit with Gehman if he would come to the Reistertown area, a suburb of Baltimore, Maryland. In February 1975, Bob Gehman moved to Reistertown, which was called at that time the fastest-growing suburb in Maryland. His wife, Carolyn, worked full time with a lawyer, and Gehman spent full time visiting from door to door. He worked in the area for four weeks before beginning the first service in March 1975, in the Reistertown elementary school. There were fifty-three in attendance. On April 25, 1975, they held the organizing service with twenty-five charter members. In a couple of years the church grew to approximately 175 in attendance and stayed at that level until the church was able to secure property and build its own facilities. The church met for six years in the school.

When Gehman looked for a permanent location, he realized most of the acreage that was advertised for sale cost more than he could afford. At this point the Lord led him to go to the county records and look for landowners in the area. Then he began going door-to-door to see if they wanted to sell any of their property. One afternoon he ran across acreage on Route 30. The farmer indicated he was going to sell to a developer. Gehman left his calling card just in case he changed his mind. Two weeks later the farmer called because he needed immediate cash. Gehman negotiated the selling price of $36,000 for seven acres, just over

$5,000 an acre, an answer to prayer because the going price in the area was over $25,000 an acre.

The church had raised $15,000 in cash but they needed to raise the remaining amount in one week. Gehman called a business meeting and asked the people to sacrifice. Within ten minutes the people had pledged the money. One elderly couple who had been charter members had $10,000 to give toward the building. The man told Gehman that he would give it for the property, realizing ground was more critical for the new church. The gentleman passed away before he could see the new building materialized. However, at the dedication of the new building, the couple was honored for their sacrificial part in getting a new church started.

The church encountered difficulty with zoning regulations before building. They had to spend $70,000 in site development. Due to the length of time in hurdling bureaucratic obstacles, many of the people got discouraged because the building was not constructed immediately. Six years after the church began, the new building was dedicated on May 5, 1981. To construct the new building a fund raiser led the church in a capital fund campaign whereby the people pledged to give $148,000 in three years. A local bank committed itself to $180,000. The building seats 300 and cost $275,000.

FAITH IS UNDERSTANDING THE WILL OF GOD AND DOING IT

When asked to define faith, Gehman said, "Faith is understanding the will of God and believing he will do it regardless of obstacles." Gehman explains that coming to Reistertown, finding the property, and constructing the building was a process of overcoming circumstances that were obstacles to him. Faith was continuing with church planting, even when he was discouraged.

A. *Faith and location.* When asked to relate faith to location, Gehman said, "I had a dream, that Dr. Falwell refers to as vision. My dream was actually an expression of my faith that led me to leave Lynchburg and come to Reistertown and plant a church." When speaking about his faith, Gehman confessed, "I had many fears; fear of failure, because I didn't have enough experience; and fear that no one would come to the first service." Gehman said, "Faith is doing what God led you to do, even when you are scared." Gehman confessed that he had some pastoral experience in serving at Thomas Road Baptist Church, but not enough experience to relieve his fears. In Lynchburg he had the support of many other church leaders. However, when he came to Reistertown, "I was on my own. I had to raise the money, create the excitement, carry through with the burden—I was the leader and had to start everything. I had to have faith for God to help me."

B. *Doctrine in faith.* To Gehman, doctrine is the foundation for the faith that he expresses in church planting. "I never once doubted that what I was preaching was truth nor did I ever once doubt that what God had said in his Word was true." He never wavered in preaching the gospel and always knew that God would use it to save lost people.

C. *Faith and objectives.* Gehman believes that the Great Commission is the ultimate objective of the church. "To me, the Great Commission is saturating the community with the gospel in an attempt to reach as many people for Jesus Christ as I could." He sees that all of his efforts to evangelize the area was an expression of faith. He says, "Soul-winning, sacrifice, and collecting money is all an act of faith." Gehman indicates, "In those early days, I am not sure whether my soul-winning sustained my personal faith or my faith toward God sustained my soul-winning." But he realized that both soul-winning and obedience to God came out of a life of faith. "Every phase of preaching requires a new step of faith, so evangelism produces faith to take more steps for God and reach larger areas of the community. I know that if I could win more souls, get them baptized in the church, and teach them to tithe, I could take a greater step of faith in buying property or a new building. Therefore faith and soul-winning go together."

D. *Methods and faith.* According to Gehman, "Saturation evangelism is the only way to build an aggressive church in a metropolitan area." He realizes at the same time, "It is impossible to saturate a large area of people when a church has such a small base of finances and workers." When he began, he could not afford newspaper, radio, or television advertisement. He confessed that for a time, "I lost sight of saturation evangelism." At the beginning, "I was winning people to Christ, but I was not saturating my community."

However, Gehman learned that there are other ways to make his community aware of the gospel. He indicates, "A young man must remain in the community for at least five years to learn how to bring his community alive to the preaching of the gospel." Now after eight years, "I am finally coming to grips with how to get the attention of my community." He tells other young pastors, "Realize that if you cannot saturate your community, don't be discouraged. Build slowly and when the church becomes large enough, it becomes easier to saturate the whole community and reach the masses for Jesus Christ."

CONCLUSION

"Faith grows when it has a correct base. People have thought they were trusting God, but their faith was based on their fantasy, which is basing your faith on your own self. When faith is based on the principles of the Word of God, faith is real, for its existence is then taken from its source.

"Our church is not further ahead because of my lack of faith. If I had greater faith when I was building the church, I could have built stronger and faster. As far as I am concerned, faith is the final foundation in all church planting and church growth."

Gehman believes the test of faith is greater in some geographical areas than in others. He believes that in the South a minister can get quicker results and attract a larger crowd. Therefore the man does not have to have great faith to build a church as in localities that are resistant to the gospel. Gehman indicated that in the North, because of the Catholics and the great amount of unchurched, it takes more faith and more work to bring them to know Jesus Christ. He says, "The spiritual coldness in the North requires the pastor to have more faith to build a new church than it does in the South where people are open to the gospel. How many cold shoulders can a young pastor take and still have faith?"

He advises that the numerical size of a church is not the measure of a man's faith, but the size of the church and its spirituality, compared to the difficulty of the field, is an adequate expression of the faith of a man. Gehman says that great faith moves great mountains, while weak faith is broken on granite boulders.

12
SPIRITUAL GIFTS
AND CHURCH GROWTH

The men who have built the largest churches in the world appear to be multi-gifted men who seemingly have extraordinary abilities. Yet, they are few in number. What about the average pastor with an average church? Can the average pastor lead his church to grow beyond its present circumstances? What gifts and abilities does the pastor need to grow a church? Also, can an average pastor develop his abilities so that he can experience greater church growth than he has thus far in his ministry?

The authors do not believe the source of church growth is luck nor finding the correct circumstances. The source of church growth does not come from a denomination, nor is it restricted to any theology. The source of church growth seems to lie within the individual, but that does not mean it is man-centered. Church growth is spiritually dynamic and has its source in God. The man who builds a church must be controlled by God in his thinking, strategy, working, and total ministry. But most of all, the man must be given abilities or spiritual gifts from God that will qualify him to produce church growth. The attitude of the man of God toward his spiritual gifts will determine the rate of growth for his church. His attitude includes finding and correctly using his gifts, then adding to his gifts and causing them to grow.

This chapter is not a complete study of spiritual gifts, but examines five words associated with spiritual gifts. These words qualify the spiritual gifts and give direction to the person who desires to understand his spiritual abilities.

These five terms are used interchangeably or explicitly in Scripture to identify spiritual gifts. They occur in the introduction to the discussion of spiritual gifts in 1 Corinthians 12 and lead to a workable definition: first, *pneumatikon* (plural) spirituals (1 Cor. 12:1); second, *charismata* (plural) gifts (1 Cor. 12:4); third, *diakonia* ministry (1 Cor. 12:5); fourth; *energeema* working (1 Cor. 12:6); and fifth, *phanerosis* manifest (1 Cor. 12:7).

1. *"Pneumatikon* spirituals." Paul advises the Christians in Corinth, "Now concerning spiritual gifts, brethren, I would not have you ignorant" (1 Cor. 12:1). He describes the gift or the ability to serve God as "spiritual." The word *gifts* is not found in the original text, but is supplied in the English translation, perhaps because the term appears in verse 4. Also the term *"pneumatika* spiritual" is found in 1 Corinthians 14:1, and again the word *gifts* is added, inferred from the context. Without the word *gift,* the term simply means "the spirituals." To understand why Paul calls our gifts "the spirituals," we must realize the word is an adjective, which gives meaning to the thing or person that possesses it. Hence, when the word *pneumatikon* is used, the author is emphasizing the spiritual nature of the gift. Therefore, the Holy Spirit, who is the source of a Christian's spirituality and who also dispenses the gift, makes the gift spiritual. Walvoord agrees:

The Greek word pneumatikon *is found in 1 Corinthians 12:1 and indicates the "things of the Spirit, i.e., spiritual gifts." The word directs attention to the source, the Holy Spirit, and the realm of these gifts.*[1]

In church growth, this does not mean that all pastors who are spiritual men in their walk with God will automatically have church growth. Remember, the gift is spiritual, not the man. But the reverse can occur; the man can be spiritual, but not have the gift. However, it seems that God would not give a spiritual gift to someone who was not spiritual. Therefore, to have church growth, the man must first become spiritual; then he must have the spiritual gifts that lead to church growth.

2. *Charismata* (gifts) is found in 1 Corinthians 12:1 and is translated "spiritual gifts." The root of the word comes from *charis,* which is "grace." Of course, grace is given freely in salvation (Eph. 2:8, 9), and when *charis* is used with spiritual gifts it implies a "gift" (freely and graciously given).[2] Hence, a spiritual gift has several implications for church growth. First, a gift comes from a source outside the receiver; hence, the ability to lead a church in growth comes from outside the pastor. Second, the gift is bestowed, which implies that the pastor must receive his ability. His attitude toward receiving his spiritual gift will reflect its effectiveness when he uses it. Finally, the attitude the receiver has toward the giver will determine his relationship to the gift itself and its use in his ministry.

3. *Diakonia* (ministry) is translated "ministries" or "administrations." A person's ministry is related to spiritual gifts. "There are differences of administrations, but the same Lord" (1 Cor. 12:5). Hence, a gift is a ministry that is given by the Lord. When the word *diakonia* is used in the context of spiritual gifts, it im-

plies that spiritual gifts are in fact spiritual ministries. Therefore, gifts are for a purpose; i.e., to be used for ministry. The verb form *diakoneo* means "to be a servant, to serve or wait upon another person, particularly to wait on tables by serving food to guests."[3] Hence, those who are given a spiritual gift should receive it with the purpose of serving other people. This implies that a spiritual gift is not received to minister primarily to oneself, nor is a spiritual gift given to serve itself. A spiritual gift is given to serve others.

In relation to church growth, a spiritual gift is never given for the sake of numerical growth alone; it is given so that the pastor can minister to people. If his gifts grow, then he can minister to more people. Church growth is never an end in itself; it is a means to an end—ministry to people.

4. Of *energeema* (operations), Paul teaches, "And there are diversities of operations, but it is the same God which worketh all in all" (1 Cor. 12:6). "Paul uses the word *energeema* to denote spiritual gifts as the activity produced by God's enduements of men for service."[4] The word from *energeo,* where we get energy, implies the power or energy of God that activates or sets something in motion. Hence, a spiritual gift is not the natural ability of the individual, but is a ministry that is empowered by God.

God gives spiritual gifts to activate church growth. The Holy Spirit, who is the source of gifts, is active in all of his ministries (leading, filling, illuminating, empowering, etc.) which work in the man of God who is doing the work of God. Next, the Holy Spirit gives him abilities (preaching, teaching, administrating, shepherding, etc.) that build the church of God. All of these operations *energize* church growth.

5. *Phanerosis* (manifestation) is used by Paul to describe a spiritual gift. "But the manifestation of the Spirit is given to every man to profit withal" (1 Cor.

12:7). Hence, a spiritual gift is a manifestation of the Holy Spirit. The word *phanerosis* comes from the verb *phaneroo*, which means "to make visible or to make clear."[5] A spiritual gift is a clear and visible manifestation of the ability of the Holy Spirit to work through the Christian even though the gift is identified as residing in the believer. When a Christian exercises a spiritual gift, it should be an evident work of the Holy Spirit. When there is church growth, it is a manifestation of the Holy Spirit who works through the man of God.

Therefore, a spiritual gift is spiritual in character *(pneumatikon)*, sovereignly given by God the Holy Spirit *(charismata)*, to others *(diakonia)*, in the power of God *(energeema)*, with an evident manifestation of the Holy Spirit through the Christian as he serves God *(phanerosis)*.

With this biblical description in mind, several definitions of spiritual gifts must be analyzed. First, a definition suggested by John R. W. Stott: "Spiritual gifts are certain capacities bestowed by God's grace and power, which fit people for specific and corresponding service."[6] Stott's definitive term is *capacity*, which means a spiritual gift is a capacity. Three observations are immediately evident from Stott's definition. First, capacities imply human ability, even though given by God. Obviously, *energeema* is God's ability working through people. Second, Stott adds human responsibility in exercising the gift. The word *diakonia* implies that a servant is entrusted with the gift and has a responsibility to use it. With that responsibility comes accountability for success or failure. Third, Stott makes the gift passive by calling it a *capacity*. But spiritual gifts are both passive to the believer (because it is God's ability) and are active from the believer (gifts have human responsibility). Stott uses the definitive term *capacity*, which implies they are passive; but the definitive term *ability* could be better used to describe spiritual gifts when referring to human responsibility.

Howard A. Snyder amplifies the definition of a spiritual gift by adding the idea of ministry:

Spiritual gifts are given not merely for personal enjoyment nor even primarily for an individual's own spiritual growth, although this too, is important. Gifts are given for the common good, "that the church may be edified" (1 Cor. 14:5).[7]

The following chart will help the reader summarize the teaching of Scripture regarding spiritual gifts.

---

1. **Source:** From the Holy Spirit.
2. **Bestowed:** To believers.
3. **Purpose:** For Christian ministry.
4. **Nature:** Spiritual ability.
5. **Discovery:** By proper relationship to the Holy Spirit.
6. **Responsibility:** To be exercised by believers.
7. **Number:** Plural.

Spiritual gifts are the various abilities given sovereignly to believers by the Holy Spirit so that when they faithfully serve the Lord, there are spiritual results. Then individuals will grow in maturity as the church grows in outreach.

13
ANSWERING QUESTIONS ABOUT SPIRITUAL GIFTS

Spiritual gifts have become the focus of investigation for many modern-day Christians. Those in the Pentecostal churches are saying all gifts are operative today, while others say that some spiritual gifts are unnecessary, hence no longer valid. Between those two positions are many views regarding gifts. These differences involve both doctrine and practice. This chapter attempts to answer some of these questions.

1. *How many gifts may a person have?* Do not think of spiritual gifts in a singular capacity, even though this book is dealing with one ministry gift: i.e., the gift of faith. What is suggested is that the gift of faith will be exercised in concert with other spiritual gifts (note the plural designation of spiritual gifts). First, the church should be a body where many gifts are operative, hence the term is plural (1 Cor. 12:4); and there are several lists of multiple gifts (Rom. 12:3-8; 1 Cor. 12:8-12, 28, 29; and Eph. 4:11). Some authors, including Gene Getz, do not refer to a plurality of gifts in the individual, but suggest there is a plurality of gifts in the church. "God's plan is a multi-gifted body, a body made up of people who could all contribute in a special

way to the building up of the church."¹ Getz then suggests that a church has more than one gift. "Rather than a multi-gifted man."² Flynn disagrees with Getz, teaching that an individual can have several gifts. He notes, "Paul's opening remarks in the section of gifts (1 Cor. 12:1-4) negates their singularity and emphasizes their plurality."³ Flynn implies one person can have two or more gifts.

When Jesus related the parable of the talents, the first servant was given five talents, the next three, and the final servant was given one. A talent in the parable is interpreted as a gift or ability, for talents are given, Jesus explains, "to every man according to his several ability" (Matt. 25:15). The servants represent multi-gifted individuals.

The word talents here is used to denote indefinitely a large sum, and is designed to refer to the endowments conferred on men. We have retained in our language the word talent as referring to the abilities or gifts of men. . . . He makes distinctions among men in regard to abilities, and in the powers and opportunities of usefulness, requiring them only to occupy those stations, and to discharge their duties there.⁴

But in the discussion of the multi-gifted person, what about the person who seems to be less gifted, as some may appear; or without a gift?⁵ Even though the word for spiritual gifts appears in the plural (1 Cor. 12:4, 31), some people may have only one gift. The apostle Peter implies a person may have only a singular gift. "As every man hath received the gift, even so minister the same one to another" (1 Pet. 4:10).

2. *What is the relationship of the spiritual gift of faith to natural ability?* A spiritual gift is not the augmented natural ability of a Christian, nor is it innate talent. From the use of *phanerosis,* a spiritual gift is the evi-

dent and manifest work of the Holy Spirit through the Christian. Leslie B. Flynn explains,

Talents instruct, inspire, or entertain on a natural level. Gifts relate to the building up of the saints (or to evangelism). Something supernatural happens in the one who is ministering when a gift is exercised. Nothing supernatural happens in one who is performing when a talent is displayed.[6]

As the spiritual gift of faith is analyzed, it cannot be described as augmented "natural faith," found in a trusting person, or a person who is generally optimistic. Yet some may confuse the natural ability to speak or teach with the spiritual gift of preaching or teaching. The gift of faith is not the power of positive thinking, nor "self-confident psychology."[7] The gift of faith is a supernatural ability whereby the person is able to win more souls to Christ or to gain a greater spiritual victory than could happen naturally.

3. *When does a person receive a spiritual gift?* Most contemporary authors are not sure when the Christian receives his spiritual gifts. Since every Christian has the Holy Spirit (Rom. 8:9), which he received at salvation, then it can be inferred that spiritual gifts came with the Holy Spirit. Also, since every Christian has a spiritual gift (1 Cor. 7:7; 1 Pet. 4:10), and the work of the Spirit regenerates a person at conversion (John 3:5; 1 Pet. 1:23), spiritual gifts could be given then. Spiritual gifts are probably bestowed at salvation. But Paul seems to imply that gifts were given earlier, at the resurrection of Christ. "When he ascended up on high, he led captivity captive, and gave gifts unto men. (Now that he ascended, what is it but that he also descended first into the lower parts of the earth? . . . that he might fill all things)" (Eph. 4:8-10). Here Paul implies that gifts were given positionally to the believer at the res-

urrection of Christ. Perhaps the answer is that God *supplied* the gifts at the resurrection, but *applies* them to believers at individual conversions (Rom. 4:25; 6:4, 5). Some suggest that God gives his gifts without partiality and that every person has the potential of developing every spiritual gift. This is because every believer has the Holy Spirit and he provides the spiritual ability. As such, a believer has the responsibility to develop the gifts and he has as many gifts as he has taken the initiative to develop.

However, experience reveals that the spiritual gifts of some are manifested at a time later in life than conversion. The answer, though only suggested in Scripture, seems to be that God gave spiritual gifts at conversion, but they lie dormant (or latent as a seed in the soil), only to come to light at a later time. Paul was converted (Acts 9), but there was a gap in time until the church at Antioch sent him as a missionary church planter, "for the work whereunto I have called [him]" (Acts 13:2).

Since human responsibility is connected with the development of gifts, perhaps some are called, but they do not immediately develop their spiritual gifts. Then later they respond to God, and their spiritual gifts are manifested.

4. *Is the gift of faith greater in some than others?* There seems to be uneven manifestation of spiritual gifts. When it comes to the gift of faith, which is the topic of this book, some people seem to trust God for greater workings of the Holy Spirit than others. Also, some seem to exercise the gift of faith more often than others. Whether this involves getting more people to pray to receive Christ, raising more money, or trusting God for greater results in church planting, the gift of faith appears to be stronger in some than others.

A spiritual gift is ministry, *diakonia* (1 Cor. 12:5), and faithfulness in ministry determines greater effectiveness (Matt. 25:23; Luke 19:17). Therefore, the person who ministers his gift with the greatest faithfulness will be more effective and will have greater results.

Paul exhorts, "Covet earnestly the best gifts" (1 Cor. 12:31), implying that *zeloute* (desire) results in a Christian's receiving the best gifts *(charismata).* At this place the word *gifts* is plural, suggesting that a Christian can receive more gifts. This implies that faithfulness in seeking and exercising a gift will lead to a greater number of gifts or a greater manifestation of one's gift. Many interpret 1 Corinthians 12:31 differently. They believe Paul is speaking to the Corinthian *corpus* (the church), not to individual believers. To prove this, they refer to the context, "Now ye are the body of Christ" (1 Cor. 12:27), as a reference to the church. Therefore, the interpretation is for the church to "covet earnestly" the higher gifts.

In other words, the church should seek leadership gifts that will minister to the corporate life of the body. Even if this interpretation is accepted, it implies the growth of spiritual gifts, which is our original argument. If the church were to seek spiritually gifted men, Paul would probably not have told them to look elsewhere for leadership, but to develop it from within the body. Whatever interpretation the reader chooses, the acquiring of a spiritual gift (its identification is not germane to the argument) is achieved by human responsibility. When properly exercised toward the proper goal, the Christian can grow in his number (quantity) of gifts and in the effectiveness (quality) of his gifts.

Jesus told the parable of the man with five talents, another with three talents, and the final man with only one talent (Matt. 25:14-30). The man with five was faithful; note two actions in the text: "He that had received five talents," implying that gifts are sovereignly given by God. Yet the same servant says, "I have gained beside them five talents more." Here human responsibility is evident and he was rewarded for his achievement. The man with three talents was faithful and received the same ratio of increase (100 percent); he worked for and received three talents. The final servant had his talent taken away and given to the man with ten talents, thus making a total of eleven talents. The parable of the talents implies that the Christian who faithfully exercises his spiritual gift of faith will grow in his ability to accomplish bigger and greater things for God. This parable also implies that a person can lose the effectiveness of his spiritual gift through disuse or unfaithfulness. Some even lose their spiritual gift altogether.

The gift of faith can become larger in effectiveness as it is exercised. Also, the one who exercises the spiritual gift of faith through his ministry may develop gifts hitherto unknown to him. While exercising faith to trust God for church growth, a person may discover the gift of evangelism so that people can be won to Christ. Or viewed another way, a person's gift of evangelism may be strengthened as he exercises the gift of faith by trusting God for more conversions. It is possible for a person to discover new spiritual gifts (discover those that appear to be latent), or strengthen his weak gifts, as he faithfully exercises his gift of faith.

5. *Can one seek the gift of faith?* The question of discovery and growth of spiritual gifts has no easy answer. First, the gifts are sovereignly given by the Holy Spirit (1 Cor. 12:4), yet Paul claims that he had part in communicating spiritual gifts to the Christians in Rome: "For I long to see you, that I may impart unto you some spiritual gift" (Rom. 1:11). Also, Paul challenged Timothy that he "Neglect not the gift that is in thee, which was given thee by prophecy, with the laying on of hands" (1 Tim. 4:14). Paul's words "by prophecy" mean "by means of," which can be interpreted that prophecy was the instrument that communicated *charismatos*. Literally, the verse could

be translated, "The in-thee spiritual gift," implying Timothy's gift was embryonic; he had it before someone developed it by preaching.

Also Paul said, "Stir up the gift of God" (2 Tim. 1:6). The word for "stir up" literally means "fan the flame." The answer lies in the Holy Spirit developing a spiritual gift in one person by using another faithful person as he ministers his gift. Timothy got his gift as he sat under the influence of the preaching of Paul. This has been called the "hot poker philosophy," meaning a young minister got his vision or compassion to win souls as he was associated with a man of God with these gifts.[8] As heat is transferred from the coals to the hot poker, so the young man becomes like those who influence him, because they have the power of suggestibility to his ministry. Whether the Holy Spirit uses one minister to motivate another to church growth, or the Holy Spirit ministers directly to another, it is a fact that both divine and human factors are evident in the communication of gifts. Charles Ryrie reinforces this view:

Although gifts are supernaturally bestowed, Paul indicates that they may be developed by the person to whom they are given. After listing some of the gifts in their order of importance he says that believers should covet the best gifts (1 Cor. 12:31). This means that an individual may be ambitious to exercise certain gifts, which ambition can only be fulfilled by study and work. Paul himself, even though he was reared on the Old Testament, needed three years in Arabia to develop his gift of teaching.

In Romans 1:11, Paul indicates that he hoped to have a part in the developing of the gifts in the churches in Rome (cf. 1 Tim. 4:14; 2 Tim. 1:6). Quite clearly others may have a part in bringing gifts to maturity and full use (cf. Eph. 4:7-12). Thus, gifts may be developed as one is ambitious in relation to self and attentive to others.[9]

6. *Is the gift of faith a prominent gift?* Even though Christian leaders have the potential of being multi-gifted, the Bible seems to teach that each man has a prominent gift—i.e., a spiritual gift that identifies his ministry, and by which the person receives identification or self-awareness. Such was Agabus, who was identified as a prophet (Acts 11:27, 28; 21:10); and Philip, who was called an evangelist (Acts 21:8). Paul seems to be referring to their prominent or unique gift by his own use of the word *idion* (proper), "Every man hath his proper gift of God" (1 Cor. 7:7). From the word *idion* we get idiomatic, "unique to one's own person." A proper gift was a person's unique ability.

Every man has his own peculiar talent, or excellence. One man excels in one thing, and another in another. One may not have this particular virtue, but he may be distinguished for another virtue quite as valuable.[10]

The question naturally follows, is the spiritual gift of faith a unique or prominent gift? Apparently no office in Scripture is designated uniquely by faith, or as prominently exercising faith; i.e., he is a "faith man." However, there are several who teach the gift of faith as foundational to all gifts, which is different from being a unique gift. To say the gift of faith is foundational for all spiritual gifts is to say it must be involved in the exercise of all other gifts, or it must be the gift used to develop all other gifts. This is saying that faith is foundational to all gifts such as preaching, teaching, administering, showing mercy, etc.

If the gift of faith is foundational, then it is not a prominent designation for those who use the gift.

Everyone could be identified or called *faithful*, as "Antipas was my faithful martyr" (Rev. 2:13). This is supported by designating all Christians by the verb form of faith, he is a believer (Acts 4:32; 13:39).

Donald Gee, writing from a Pentecostal perspective, maintains that the gift of faith is foundational: "It is significant that faith comes in this group (gifts of power) as being fundamental to the other gifts of power."[11] By this context, Gee says that healing and miracles are exercises of faith, which also is a power gift.

John of St. Thomas, writing from a Roman Catholic orientation, indicates that there are seven gifts, which he describes as a "plurality of gifts."[12] He does not attempt to prove that a person may have more than one, but states that "Since Scripture asserts that the gifts are actually more than one, no further proof is needed."[13] Then he implies that the gift of faith is foundational to the others, "For through faith, the very existence of these gifts is made known."[14] He continues, "For faith attains to very many things."[15] Yet, he does not say that faith is the same thing as the other gift, nor does he make faith a part of the other gifts. Faith is separate from the other gifts, but functions through and with them.

Faith can no more perform the functions of the gifts of wisdom and understanding than they could accomplish those of faith. Each operates within its own sphere. Faith believes in God revealing without involving itself in inquiry or judgment.... It performs no operation other than that of believing, although it may be concerned with more objects than some of the gifts and fewer than others.... Each gift taken separately extends to many objects but not to the exercise of the function of any other gift.[16]

But there are others who are convinced that the gift of faith has a separate function, other than being foundational to the other gifts. Most Pentecostals recognize Harold Horton's *The Gifts of the Spirit* as a classic in the field which represents their point of view. He states,

The gift of faith is erroneously regarded as the basis of all the other Gifts of the Spirit. This is to confuse the different kinds of faith. Faith (what I have above called "general faith") is certainly necessary to the operation of all the Gifts, even the operation of the Gift of Faith; but the Gift of Faith is a supernatural endowment quite distinct from this "general faith," and equally distinct from the other eight supernatural endowments of the Spirit.[17]

7. *What is the relationship between a church office and the gift of faith?* A spiritual gift is not the same as an office in the church. Most Protestant churches recognize two offices: pastors and deacons (Phil. 1:1); but other groups recognize such church offices as prophets, teachers, bishops, etc. A spiritual gift is a supernatural endowment or ability given by the Holy Spirit. Yet a man can desire more gifts (1 Cor. 12:31). Also, a man can desire an office in the church: "If a man desire the office of a bishop" (1 Tim. 3:1). This section reveals that men who seek the office must have certain qualifications, presumably so the congregation can recognize those who should be placed in the office.

There is a relationship between gift and office, or between ability and position. The person who has the office of bishop/elder (1 Tim. 3:1-10) should have the gift of pastor (Eph. 4:11). The one who holds the office of deacon (1 Tim. 3:11-14) should also possess the gift of serving or ministering *(diakonia;* we get the title deacon from the word for serving). In the same manner, those who believe in the office of the prophet (1 Cor. 12:10) and those who advocate the office of evangelist (Eph. 4:11) should require that the person who fills them have the gift of prophecy and evangelism. Flynn has summarized this view:

Naturally, a person with an office should have the gift corresponding to that office; otherwise his office will be in name only . . . summing up, a believer would not hold a divinely appointed office without possessing the corresponding gift.[18]

However, the opposite may not be true; that is, a person may have the gift without the office related to it. Flynn also holds the view that "many Christians possess a gift without appointment to that office."[19] These might be people who have the gift of serving, *diakonos,* without serving in the office of deacon. Also, a person may have the gift of shepherding without being a pastor. The authors teach that "A Sunday school teacher is the extension of the pastor's responsibilities into the Sunday school class. . . . Everything a pastor is to his flock, the teacher is to his/her class."[20] Therefore, those who shepherd a Sunday school class are exercising a gift similar to those who shepherd a congregation.

The spiritual gift of faith does not seem to have a corresponding office. There seems to be no one who is called uniquely to exercise faith in the church, apparently because there is no such office identified in Scripture. Also, no such office has arisen in the church over the years, nor is there a unique identifiable ministry of exercising faith, as there is a unique ministry of preaching, teaching, or evangelizing.

8. *What is the relationship between ministries and the gift of faith?* Flynn suggests that "gifts are not

ministries."[21] As such he identifies a ministry as "an
outlet for employment of a gift."[22] A ministry may be
to an age group such as adults or youth; it may be
through media such as radio, television, or Bible college; or it may be at home or on the foreign mission
field. Flynn also identifies ministries as music, writing, or linguistics.[23] Ryrie also believes that spiritual
gifts are not ministries.

*Neither does Paul suggest that there are special gifts
for specific age groups. There is no gift of young people's work, for all ages need teachers, pastors, helpers,
etc. (cf. Titus 2:1-8). The gift is the ability, according
to Paul's thinking, and not the place or age group in
which that ability is used.[24]*

There is apparently no unique ministry attached to
exercising faith. As a result, there seems to be no
point in time when a church would call for a person
to employ specifically the spiritual gift of faith. In
times of need a church would call for a revivalist, and
at other times a church would call for a Bible teacher.
After the same manner—but to meet a different
need—a church would call for someone to train them
in Sunday school education or lead them in evangelism. But the church apparently does not call for a
person who has the unique gift of faith. Rather, faith
meets a general need, or is involved in meeting all
needs. When the Bible teacher, evangelist, or foreign
missionary comes to meet a unique need at a church,
he must exercise the gift of faith (as said before, this
gift is separate, yet exercised in connection with other
gifts), while he exercises his dominant gift. Also, the
church is exercising faith in calling for a unique ministry (perhaps not the gift of faith). In summary, Flynn
has observed, "The specialty sphere, or area in which

a gift is exercised constitutes a ministry. There a ministry is not a gift."[25]

9. *What is the relationship between the fruit of the Spirit and the gift of faith?* "The word faith is listed both as a spiritual gift (Rom. 12:3, 6; 1 Cor. 12:9) and the fruit of the Spirit."[26] A spiritual gift is an ability to be used in service, where spiritual fruit relates to a Christian's character. It is possible to have spiritual gifts to serve God, but to be lacking in spiritual character. (The Corinthians had several gifts, but were guilty of envy, divisions, and fleshly sins.) Also, it is possible to have spirituality, yet not manifest many or all spiritual gifts. "Are all apostles? are all prophets? are all teachers? are all workers of miracles?" (1 Cor. 12:29).

When considering the gift of faith, it is possible to have enough faith to move mountains, yet lack love (1 Cor. 13:2). Flynn describes this person: "Possession of gifts does not indicate godliness of life."[27] This probably does not mean the person is ungodly, nor is he void of love; it means the gift of faith that moves mountains is not tied to the fruit of love. Three possible conclusions may be drawn. First, the person has not grown in love as he has grown in exercising his gift of faith. Second, the exercise of the two has different objects; faith is toward God, while love is toward others. Third, love is a manifestation of the Holy Spirit (1 Cor. 12:7).

But what about the relationship between the spiritual gift of faith and the spiritual fruit of faith? They are not the same, even though they both probably came with the baptism of the Spirit (1 Cor. 12:13) and have their source from the Holy Spirit. They are related as the gift of faith and the fruit of love were seen in the previous paragraph. The fruit of faith is the believer's attitude of living daily by faith, "For we walk by faith, not by sight" (2 Cor. 5:7). Therefore, all believers can have the fruit of faith to live the Christian life, whereas the spiritual gift of faith is sovereignly bestowed upon recipients to serve Christ through the church.

But, obviously there is a congruence to gifts and fruit, even if there is no cause and effect relationship. Those who have a godly life (spiritual fruit) will be closer to God, so they may trust him more fully for answers to prayer. Those who are godly will probably have a clearer vision of what God wants to perform in a certain situation. (Since sin will blind or dull the vision of the saint, those who are godly will see a greater potential that can be accomplished for God.) Then, because of the spiritual fruit in their lives, they can better exercise the spiritual gift of faith in conjunction with other spiritual gifts.

To summarize spiritual fruit, it: (1) is given to all believers; (2) produces spiritual character; (3) is singular (fruit is singular, meaning one's character is a unit); (4) is permanent (1 Cor. 13:8-10); and (5) grows internally. To summarize spiritual gifts, note the contrast to the previous five points. Spiritual gifts: (1) are given to specific believers; (2) produce spiritual service; (3) are plural (Flynn lists nineteen, Wagner, twenty-seven); (4) will cease; and (5) operate externally.

10. *What is the relationship between daily faith and the gift of faith?* The spiritual gift of faith is not the same as living by faith,[28] as Kinghorn observes; "While all Christians possess the grace of faith, not all Christians possess the gift of faith."[29] Koch separates the gift of faith from justifying faith, "When faith is mentioned in the list of gifts of the Spirit, this does not mean the justifying faith that everyone must have who believes for eternal life. The faith that comes as a gift of the Spirit is the daring and conquering faith

that 'removes mountains.' "[30] Harold Carter distinguished, "The gift of faith is a wonderful gift that has not been fully understood, we fear, because it is generally confused with ordinary faith, or serving faith."[31] B. E. Underwood notes of the spiritual gift of faith that it "is not the ordinary faith of the believer."[32] Therefore, Gee concludes, "The spiritual gift of faith must be distinguished from ordinary faith."[33] Flynn makes the observation, "The gift of faith, listed by Paul in 1 Corinthians 12:9, is more than saving faith."[34] Therefore, the conclusion is that the spiritual gift of faith is: (1) not synonymous with saving faith; (2) even though it is generally confused with saving faith; but (3) is more than saving faith; and (4) is built on daily faith.

The spiritual gift of faith has been generally described as "faith of miracles"[35] by Gee, who quotes older theologians, "special faith"[36] in *The Living Bible's* paraphrase of 1 Corinthians 12:9, "Wonderworking faith"[37] by Underwood, "daring faith"[38] by Koch, and "the gift of prayer"[39] by John MacArthur. All of these titles indicate that the gift of faith is special. As Friesen describes it, "The gift of faith is rather a special God-given ability."[40]

But even when the authors who write about the gift of faith recognize that it is special, they do not generally agree on a definition. Perhaps their disagreement arises from the fact that (1) little is said of the gift of faith in Scripture; (2) the church has largely ignored the gift of faith and its practice; or (3) Christian writers have not researched the topic thoroughly.

CONCLUSION

The person who seeks the gift of faith probably has the desire because God has sovereignly and latently given him the gift. He may seek the gift of faith scrip-turally, and he should allow himself to be influenced by those with faith. But first he should develop his personal faith, which is the fruit of the Spirit, by grounding himself in Scripture and prayer. He should recognize that the gift of faith will probably not be his dominant gift, but that it can grow (Luke 17:6). It may grow in others more than in his life. Finally, the gift of faith is a serving ability that will become more effective as the person trusts God, follows his direc-tion, and aggressively serves Jesus Christ.

THE GIFT OF FAITH

As mentioned in the Introduction, there seem to be three different approaches to understanding and interpreting the gift of faith, yet apart from this book, no one has used these classifications.

First, there are those who interpret the serving gift of faith as an instrument that can be used in Christian service as one would use the Bible, the gift of administration, or the gift of preaching to accomplish the work of God. This is the *instrumental* view, which appears to be the traditional or historical view. It is listed first because of its historical priority.

Second, the gift of faith is interpreted as the ability to see or perceive what God desires to accomplish. The person with the gift of faith sees what God wants accomplished, then uses every resource available to complete the project. This is called the *insight* or *vision* view, because the gift of faith is seeing what God can do in a situation. This second view seems to be the recent interpretation held by most evangelical Christians now writing on spiritual gifts.

Third, the gift of faith is the ability to move God to divinely intervene in the work so that God accomplishes what the person with the gift believes will happen. This view is called the *interventional* interpretation. This view is held mostly by Pentecostals, who believe that miracles are presently occurring in the work of God. It is also held by some pastors identified with large churches (plus other leaders with dynamically growing works) who believe the day of miracles has passed, yet they have experienced the intervention of God in their Christian service.

Perhaps the three interpretations of the gift of faith are three progressive steps in expressing faith in God. The three views are different points on a continuum. Those who believe the first step, *instrumental* faith, have used faith as an instrument (Eph. 6:16), but they do not necessarily deny the work of God in the next two steps. They just have not grown or continued to a higher level of usefulness. The same can be said of the second interpretation, *insight* faith, for they have used faith as a vision to see what God can accomplish. The third position does not interpret the gift of faith differently, but includes the first two aspects, then adds the *interventional* factor.

1. *The gift of faith as an instrument.* The gift of faith is interpreted to be the ability of the Christian to use the instrument of Christianity to carry out the work of God in a person or in a church. In Ephesians, Paul describes the Christian who fights the enemy with faith and other instruments. He uses truth (v. 14), righteousness (the knowledge of imputed perfection, v. 14), the gospel (v. 15), the helmet of salvation (v. 17), and the sword which is the Word of God (v. 17). He defends himself with the shield of faith (v. 16), an instrument.

Howard Carter, a Pentecostal, says, "The gift of faith can be defined as faith imparted by the Spirit of God for protection in times of danger, or for divine provision, or it may include the ability to impart blessing."[1] This definition does not include insight nor the intervention of God. The gift of faith includes the ministries that God has already promised, such as protection, provision, and blessing. Later, Carter describes the gift of faith with more intentionality. "This remarkable gift brings into operation the powers of the world to come; it causes God to work for you."[2]

John of St. Thomas, the Roman Catholic, suggested a traditional view in his discussion of the gift of faith: "Faith believes in God ... without involving itself in inquiry or judgment concerning matters of faith. It performs no operation other than that of believing."[3]

Instrumental faith would be available to all believers, not just a few gifted individuals who build large churches or accomplish great projects for God.

Also, the instrumental view would make faith a response to or an ability to use the Word of God. This says nothing about the gift of faith uniquely giving a vision of service or solving a crisis or unique problems. The instrumental view is more conformable to a historic Protestant view: i.e., that the day of miracles has passed. Miracles are viewed as a demonstration of authority to validate the message from God; hence, there is no longer a need for miracles because the content of revelation is complete (Jude 3). This also implies that God does not supernaturally intervene in the affairs of life, but rather he works through the means of grace (the instruments, including faith) that he has already supplied. Therefore, the interventional gift of faith is viewed by some as having properties similar to a miracle, hence not applicable to this age of grace.

The instrumental approach takes a passive view of the person with the gift of faith. It sees both the person and his gift as channels or vehicles used by God. God has placed power within the Scriptures (Heb. 4:12; James 1:17; 2 Pet. 1:4), and the Holy Spirit (Acts 1:8). Power (including the instrumental gift of faith) is not resident within the human, for he is an earthen vessel

(2 Tim. 2:21). Power is of God, not man. The Christian accomplishes the work of God through the Word of God, by the Holy Spirit who indwells him. Only in this manner is the person an instrument to accomplish what God has promised.

Perhaps those who hold the instrumental view see God controlling the destiny of this world (their extreme predestination has led to fatalism); therefore, they reject the interventional view because they believe man cannot change the predetermined order of events by his faith. To them faith is only instrumental, and they leave the results to the will of God. Thus they have not been aggressive (interventional) in changing the natural course or the general affairs of men, and they lack initiative in the work of God.

Others might view the gift of faith as passive because they relate the gift of faith to other ministries. They feel spiritual gifts are given to men: i.e., preachers, teachers, evangelists, etc. (Eph. 4:11). God works through men who are identified by their gift; i.e., prophets have the gift of prophecy , teachers have the gift of teaching, etc. But there is no ministry identified with the gift of faith, such as a "faither." Therefore, they see God working in the world through secondary sources, such as through his laws, the influence of his Word, the Holy Spirit, and the affairs of life. They do not see the gift of faith as an intervention by God in an active or direct role, but rather the gift of faith is an instrumental or indirect (secondary) role.

2. *The gift of faith as insight.* The gift of faith is the Holy Spirit giving the Christian the ability to see (envision) what God desires to perform, or is able to perform regarding a project. After the Christian perceives what can be accomplished, he dedicates himself to its accomplishment. Perhaps the best known definition is suggested by Peter Wagner, who states, "The gift of faith is the special ability that God gives to some mem-

bers of the Body of Christ to discern with extraordinary confidence the will and purposes of God for the future of His work."[4]

The strength of this definition is in the Christian's ability to see what God can do in a given situation; hence it is implied that the Christian must see God's nature and purpose, and that is understood only through his Word. Kinghorn supports this second insight approach by stating, "The gift of faith is given to some Christians as a special ability to see the adequacy of God and to tap it for particular situations."[5] To this definition, Flynn adds that the gift of faith not only sees potentials but overcomes obstacles. "The gift of faith is a Spirit-given ability to see something that God wants done and to sustain unwavering confidence that God will do it, regardless of seemingly insurmountable obstacles."[6]

The insight view recognizes that God is the source of all Christian work, but the person who exercises faith senses his responsibility to carry out the project. This view places a high degree of responsibility and accountability on man. God is active in giving vision, but man is passive in receiving the vision; then he allows God to work through him to accomplish this project. This view implies that the work of God is accomplishing this project. It also implies that the work of God is accomplished in relationship to the ability of the worker—including man's knowledge, wisdom, motivational powers, leadership ability, etc. Of course, God gave these abilities to men, but God gave them through secondary means (training, reading, "hot poker," etc.) and God works through them by secondary means.

Wagner describes Robert Schuller, pastor of Crystal Cathedral, Garden Grove, California, as a man with the gift of faith. He describes Schuller's vision of a building larger than Notre Dame Cathedral of Paris, of 10,000 pieces of glass shaped like diamonds, and fountains of water down the center aisle. Wagner says, "Before I heard about his vision, I had already come to the conclusion that God had given him the gift of faith."[7]

The gift of faith may be the supernatural ability of a person to determine what God will do in a church in the next ten years, or at any future date. As a result, those who have the gift of faith are (1) growth-oriented, (2) goal-oriented, (3) optimistic, and (4) confident.[8] Some people with natural faith may display the above four aspects and build a chain-store empire or a multimillion-dollar business. These characteristics result in the power of positive thinking. The cause is the spiritual gift of faith or vision; the result is a confident attitude that usually produces results in the work of God. Because this gift has become such a strong conviction with the pastor and he can communicate his vision to the congregation, they will work and sacrifice to accomplish the project.

Perhaps a problem with the insight view is that it makes faith synonymous with vision, which might imply that faith is a passive gift. But faith seems to be active and is used by God to change circumstances. Yet no one could honestly deny that vision is inherent in faith. In saving faith, a person must see his sin, see God, and see the remedy that God has provided in the gospel. In serving faith, a person must incorporate the role of the seer/prophet (1 Sam. 9:9) which is seeing the need first, seeing farthest into the future, and seeing the greatest thing that God could accomplish in any situation.[9] Perhaps the gift of faith not only incorporates vision, but goes to the next aspect in which the man of God intervenes in the circumstances of life.

3. *The gift of faith as intervention.* The gift of faith is the ability to move God to intervene divinely in a crisis that is facing a project, or change the expected order of events so that the work of God goes forward. This view holds that the gift of faith is active, and the

person is responsible, but God is the source of the gift and the source of accomplishment. Traditionally called the gift of miracles,[10] it features divine intervention in a miraculous way.

The leader usually has divine certainty that God will intervene (perhaps because of insight); hence, he makes an expression of faith. Gee explains,

The spiritual gift of faith is a special quality of faith, sometimes called by our older theologians the "faith of miracles." It would seem to come upon certain of God's servants in times of special crisis or opportunity in such mighty power that they are lifted right out of the realm of even natural and ordinary faith in God— and have a divine certainty put within their soul that triumphs over everything. It is a magnificent gift and is probably exercised frequently with far-reaching results.[11]

Underwood's definition is not as long, but implies the same elements: "This is extraordinary wonder-working faith for a particular occasion."[12]

Harold Horton clearly indicates that the initiation of moving the mountain begins with man exercising the gift of faith. "The Gift of faith is a supernatural endowment by the Spirit whereby that which is offered or desired by man, or spoken by God, shall eventually come to pass."[13] The verse often quoted in connection with the interventional view is the one that links speaking and exercising faith. "Whosoever shall say unto this mountain, Be thou removed, and be thou cast into the sea; and shall not doubt in his heart, but shall believe that those things which he saith shall come to pass; he shall have whatsoever he saith" (Mark 11:23, 24). Three times Jesus admonished his disciples to say exactly what they wanted to happen, telling them they would get the results they sought.

The author Towns has coined the phrase "Say-It-Faith" to express this aspect of the gift of faith. The book *Say-It-Faith* gives several illustrations in the ministry of the author Falwell in which he says publicly that a crisis will be solved or that an unbelievable project will be attempted and completed.

Earlier the objection was raised that the interventional view made the gift of faith similar to the gifts of miracles, tongues, and healings, which are called the power gifts or a manifestation of supernatural phenomena in today's world. Horton answers the objection,

The operation of miracles is more an act, as when the waters were opened by Moses and Elijah; while the operation of the gift of faith is more a process. . . . Faith the gift is equally miraculous with all the other Gifts, but we might say that its power or manifestation is of greater duration than those of the Gifts of Healing or Miracles.[14]

So, the third view is interventional faith, which is an ability given by the Holy Spirit whereby a person changes the events in a normal ministry, so that the work of God goes forward.

OBSERVATIONS OF INTERVENTIONAL FAITH

1. *Interventional faith goes beyond the normal instrument of faith that is available for Christian work in the present world.* Interventional faith is involved in intercessory prayers, but is "abundantly more" than God answering prayers. Those who exercise interventional faith pray, but the gift of faith is more than a prayer of faith (James 5:14), or to "ask in faith" (James 1:6). God seems to give them unexpected re-

sults because they exercise faith whether or not they pray. Sometimes interventional faith is exercised through prayer; at other times, the Christian will accomplish results by saying to a mountain, "Be thou removed" (Mark 11:23).

2. *Interventional faith is more than living by faith* (Hab. 2:4; Rom. 1:17; Gal. 3:11; Heb. 11:38; 2 Cor. 5:7). When a Christian is living by faith, he is applying the principles of the Word of God to his life with the result that he lives a godly life that is pleasing to the Lord. Living by faith involves the personal life of the believer as he exercises trust in the Lord. But in contrast, interventional faith involves Christian service in ministry for Christ. The Christian exercises faith to change the circumstances (solve a problem, supply a need, stop a force, or provide protection) so that the work of God goes forward.

3. *Interventional faith goes beyond the normal biblical methods and principles available to the church.* God has provided that certain principles should be followed in Christian work, such as: (a) going to people (Mark 16:15); (b) being a witness (Acts 1:8); (c) gathering people together (Deut. 31:12); and (d) praying for God's blessing on the work (Acts 4:31). These and other principles are available for Christian work, but there are times and circumstances when the work of God is halted. The normal principles of Christianity are applied, but the barriers or problems (called mountains, Mark 11:23) continue to face the work of God. At this time, a person with the spiritual gift of faith can exercise it to remove the problem or to change circumstances. At times, the gift of faith is exercised simultaneously with other ministries and the outside observer may mistakenly think something other than faith has solved the problem. As an illustration, first a person may exercise faith to cause a church to grow. Second, the person uses advertise-

ment, or displays powerful preaching to motivate people to invite their neighbors to attend church. The attendance problem is solved and the primary solution has come through the exercise of faith. The secondary solution has come through motivational preaching and proper use of advertising.

4. *Interventional faith is related to circumstances that lead to a solution of a problem or changing circumstances.* A pastor may exercise faith to build a new auditorium, yet the congregation has no apparent finances available. God could give the church a large gift or someone could die and leave the church enough in the bequest for construction of new facilities. There are many illustrations whereby God used ordinary circumstances in response to the exercise of faith, so that unexpected timing or unexpected sources provided solutions to the problems in a church. In each case there was an unusual intervention by God, even though he used secondary sources.

5. *Interventional faith may solve a problem or alter circumstances apart from the expected flow of things.* God may solve a church's problem through such an outstanding display of events that observers may interpret the solution to be supernatural or miraculous. However, the miraculous is only perceptual. This could be the outpouring of money from such a large number of people (including those not expected to give) that the supply is labeled "a divine supply."

6. *Interventional faith goes beyond the normal tools that Christians use in Christian service.* These tools, also called "means of grace" by sacramental churches, are the influence of the Bible, the Holy Spirit's work (conviction, illumination, guiding, filling, or empowering), the influence of a godly life, the ministry gifts (preaching, teaching, counseling, etc.), the use of the church office (pastor and deacons), the use of baptism and the Lord's Table, or involvement in the church by attendance, service, and fellowship.

When a person exercises the gift of faith, he does more than obey the Lord in the employment of the above named "tools" or "means of grace." The exercise of the gift of faith is an intentional effort on the part of the person who desires to change the circumstances of the work of God or solve a perplexing problem. At times, the person may do two or more things at one time, such as motivate people to be baptized, yet his exercise of faith is evident in that people are scripturally baptized. His faith and preaching may bring revival to the church, or become evident when many people carry out the Great Commission in their neighborhood. To one it may be an evident display of faith, to the next it is a primary desire to get people to obey God (because of great confidence that God will move hearts to be baptized), and yet the person may not be aware that he is exercising the gift of faith.

7. *Interventional faith is not always dependent upon exact doctrine or mature knowledge of doctrine.* The author Towns has interviewed the pastors of the ten largest churches in America, and the ten largest in the world.[15] He has reported his conversations with Dr. Yonggi Cho, pastor of the Full Gospel Church, Seoul, Korea, and with Dr. Jack Hyles, pastor of First Baptist Church, Hammond, Indiana. Dr. Cho told Towns the primary reason for the spectacular growth of his church was the baptism of the Holy Ghost, resulting in an enduement of power, eradication of the old man, and speaking in tongues. Dr. Jack Hyles denies the biblical interpretation of the Pentecostal experience and does not believe tongues are for this dispensation. Obviously, one or both men have painted the other (or themselves) into a theological corner. Who is right? The answer to this question, along with the correct view of other controversial issues, does not seem to be a factor in the exercise of the gift of faith.

The author believes both Dr. Cho and Dr. Hyles are

filled with the power of the Holy Spirit and that God is blessing both churches in spite of the fact that they radically disagree in their approach to the Holy Spirit. But both men believe in the fundamentals of Christianity. The term "blessability" justifies the apparent conflict. God blesses those who place themselves in a positive position to God's formula that brings success in church work. God does not punish his workers, nor annul their usefulness for wrong doctrine until their variance negates their positive influence. God blesses those who put themselves into a place to be blessed.

Those who have the gift of faith transcend doctrinal boundaries. As a matter of fact, God's blessing is not based on being doctrinally literate, correct, or complete. The new babe in Christ can exercise faith and "move mountains"; all he needs is "faith as a grain of mustard seed" (Matt. 17:20).

On the other side of the issue, the greatest display of faith is by those who have grown in their exercise of faith, so that they are more mature in Christ. Of course, maturity is dependent upon growth in doctrine and understanding.

Then, too, there probably is a limit to the tolerance by God of false doctrine. Perhaps God condescends to those who hold differing doctrines until a person accumulates too much doctrinal static or interference for him to be identified as a Bible Christian and his doctrinal weakness limits his effectiveness for service. Probably God has his "point of counterproductivity" so that when a person crosses an invisible point of no return, God no longer responds to the person's exercise of faith. Considered in God's denial of this person's faith is his yieldedness to truth, pursuit of truth, and attitude to those of another doctrinal persuasion.

8. *Interventional faith should not be confused with*

holiness of life nor separation from sin. Those who feel that the blessing of God depends upon the separation of the person from sin are perplexed when they hear that another person they thought was a Christian is engaged in something they call "sin." From God's perspective, no person is ever completely separated from sin. As soon as a yielded Christian deals with a sin in his life, God seems to reveal another issue for him to deal with. The Christian life is continual sanctification, which leads to continual victory over sin. Since the Christian life is a continuum, the question could be asked, "At what point in the continuum does the person become pure enough to exercise interventional faith?" Obviously, there is no point where the gift of faith begins its operation. When the person begins his ministry, faith may be exercised in a small capacity. A person may grow in the gift of faith as old habits and sins are pruned by the Holy Spirit. Even though the two actions are separate, they have a correlation through maturity and total experiences.

God does not bless a person's ministry because of legalism, nor does a person have the gift of faith because of cleaning up his life. Some may claim that repentance of a particular sin is a criterion for God's interventional activity in their church work. They are wrong; it is faith that motivates God to intervene in the circumstances of a church. However, some have repented of certain sins, hoping that, by the exercise of "cleaning up their life," God would intervene in their church work. Obviously, repentance can lead to greater faith, but repentance is not what moves God to work in a church. God is pleased by faith (sometimes expressed in repentance) and blesses the church because of faith. God has recognized the act of faith and solves problems, so that the work of God goes forward. But the repentance was not the causal

factor that brought about the result, i.e., the intervention of God; the cause was faith.

9. *Interventional faith seems to be related to Christian service in the church, rather than to be available
for the Christian to intervene in the general affairs of
life.* The spiritual gifts are for spiritual ministry; as
such they are the manifestation of the Holy Spirit
(1 Cor. 12:7). Some believers have taken a step of faith
in their businesses, then prayed for God's blessing on
their company. Perhaps some have taken a loan as a
step of faith; nevertheless, due to circumstances outside their control, they went bankrupt. We cannot
examine the integrity of the person, nor his business.
But good Christians have worked hard and their businesses have failed. What is the relationship of a Christian's personal life or business life to the gift of faith?
Obviously, if he lives by daily faith, he is obeying the
Bible. That obedience gives him added help in his
business life. But, when viewing the gift of faith, it
does not seem related to business life, but to Christian
ministry. God gives gifts to Christians (1 Cor. 7:7;
1 Pet. 4:10), and then states in the chapter on spiritual
gifts, "Now ye are the body of Christ, and members
in particular. And God hath set some in the church,
first apostles" (1 Cor. 12:27, 28). Since these gifts are
mentioned within the context of the church, it seems
they are related to its ministry. Also, Paul advised the
Ephesians that some gifts are given "for the perfect-
ing of the saints, for the work of the ministry, for the
edifying of the body of Christ" (Eph. 4:12).

It is questionable whether the gift of faith can or
should be exercised in relationship to secular activities. If it is interventional faith, we might question
whether God would intervene in the secular business,
even if it is owned by a Christian. However, the relationship between sacred and secular business is

sometimes a gray area. Also, since gifts build up Christians, God might use the exercise of a gift in business to edify a Christian. Thus a Christian may exercise faith in his business, and as a result, his gift would grow in usefulness and he would be more effective in his church or Christian service.

10. *Interventional faith is based on and grows out of using faith as a vision and using faith as an instrument.* Although interventional faith is similar to the two previous positions, interventional faith is initiated by those who have the unique gift of faith. The three views of the spiritual gift of faith indicate that there are differences in interpreting the biblical data. But in all three, power comes from God and the accomplishments come from God.

THREE VIEWS OF THE GIFT OF FAITH

NAME	INITIATION	VISION	POWER	ACCOMPLISHMENT	AVAILABLE
1. Instrumental	God	God	God	by God	to all
2. Insight	God	person**	God	by God	to chosen
3. Interventional	person*	person**	God	by God	to chosen

*God is the source of all Christian work, but by exercising the gift of faith, the man of God senses his responsibility for church growth and uses faith to carry it out.

**God gives a vision through his Word for all Christian work, but in the exercise of the gift of faith, the man of God perceives a particular project in time and place.

Many practical questions have been raised and possible solutions have been presented. So that none may view this chapter as academic with no relationship to the ministry, the next section deals with the application of the gift of faith to ministry.

APPLICATION OF
THE GIFT OF FAITH

The gift of faith must now be analyzed for its practical implication, especially its influence on church growth. The following observations are made on the basis established previously that the gift of faith is ministry-oriented, can grow in usefulness, and is exercised in relation to human responsibility.

1. *Announce a solution to problems facing the ministry.* Jesus advised his disciples to "Say unto this mountain, Be thou removed" (Mark 11:23). Since a mountain was a barrier or obstacle to the work of God, a first step in removing problems in the Lord's work is to say what is desired. Paul described this process, "and though I have all faith, so that I could remove mountains" (1 Cor. 13:2). This seems to be an illustration that the early church understood; i.e., that they were to remove problems by a statement that reflected their faith that God would solve the problems.

Paul made statements that God would solve problems that faced him. Paul announced that the boat should not leave Crete: "Ye should have harkened unto me, and not have loosed from Crete" (Acts 27:21). He further publicly announced the results that he expected from God: "I exhort you to be of good cheer: for there shall be no loss of any man's life among you" (Acts 27:22). Finally, Paul attached a statement of faith to his public announcement, "For I believe God, that it shall be even as it was told me" (Acts 27:25). This illustration is not explicitly entitled an exercise of the gift of faith, but it surely is an implication of faith. Some might explain that Paul spoke in faith because the angel appeared to him the previous night (Acts 27:23). But the angel confirmed what Paul had previously communicated as a statement of faith in solution to the problem. Hence, the situation has all the characteristics of one who exercises faith to announce a solution to the problem.

2. *Setting goals or announcing specific plans for the ministry.* The gift of faith involves a continuum with three points. First, relying on the instruments of God to accomplish the ministry; second, having vision to see what God could accomplish; and third, motivating God to intervene so the work will prosper. These three aspects are practically applied by setting goals for church growth or making specific plans that will prosper the ministry and produce growth. Paul planned to visit the churches in Greece to receive an offering and take it to Jerusalem. "Now concerning the collection for the saints, as I have given order to the churches of Galatia, even so do ye" (1 Cor. 16:1a). There was no qualification in the plan such as, "if you have the money," nor did Paul have a contingency plan, "if the money comes in." Paul made a confident statement that the money would be received; and "them will I send to bring your liberality unto Jerusalem" (1 Cor. 16:3).

In church growth, the leader must believe that his goal is biblical, then publicly announce with confidence what can be expected. Stevens has noted in *The Theology of the New Testament,* "Now faith is a firm confidence with respect to the objects of hope, an assured conviction of the existence of invisible realities."[16]

The illustrations of faith in Hebrews 11 reflect those who made plans and acted upon them. Noah built an ark (v. 7); Abraham went into an unknown country (v. 8); the parents of Moses preserved his life (v. 23); and Moses rejected Egypt to choose life with Israel (vv. 24-27). Stevens identifies these illustrations with intervening faith:

For our author, faith is no mere intellectual faith. It is a living and intense conviction of the supernatural which evidences in conduct. Its most characteristic effort is heroism. It is faith which "moves mountains" of difficulties and improbability.[17]

Of course, the ministry has prospered where people did not set goals, make specific plans, nor exercise faith. Such was the case when God delivered Peter from prison. Apparently, the people were not praying in faith because the church seemed surprised and even doubted that Peter was released (Acts 12:15). In many such cases, God seems to work in spite of the lack of faith of Christians.[18]

Also, Paul announced at least one goal that apparently was not accomplished. "Whensoever I take my journey into Spain" (Rom. 15:24). Later, this study will analyze men who announced attendance goals that were not met. Therefore, there are several cautions a leader should note when exercising the gift of faith to announce goals or solutions to problems. Paul may have spoken in self desire, and some who set goals for church growth may do so for human motives, not under divine guidance.

But, on the other hand, perhaps the gift of faith works through the leader's desire concerning church growth goals. He is simply articulating what God desires to accomplish. Perhaps the goals are accomplished by someone else, or are accomplished later in life, or after the leader dies. As an illustration, Paul apparently did not go to Spain, but the gospel was carried there by others. In any case, the leader must never assume omniscience. Everything he says may not be said by faith, and what he says may not be the will of God. James warns the Christian, "Go to now, ye that say, To day or to morrow we will go into such a city, and continue there a year, and buy and sell, and get gain" (James 4:13). James cautions, "Ye ought to say, If the Lord will, we shall live, and do this, or that" (James 4:15). Whenever a leader exercises the gift of faith and states a goal or announces specific plans, he ought to do so with the attitude that everything is qualified by the will of God. Since the will of God is reflected in the Word of God, the goals and plans that are closest to Scripture are closest to the will of God.

3. *A positive attitude in the ministry.* If the leader exercises faith in the proper way, then he will have confidence in God. The writer of Hebrews observed, "Now faith is being sure of what we hope for and certain of what we do not see" (Heb. 11:1, NIV). When this attitude is carried into Christian service, the leader will minister with confidence. Paul announced, "I can do all things through Christ which strengtheneth me" (Phil. 4:13). This confidence was based on the power of Christ, and is not explicitly related to the gift of faith. At another place, he confidently notes, "Thanks be unto God, which always causeth us to triumph in Christ" (2 Cor. 2:14). In both of the above references, there is not a direct traceable cause-and-effect relationship between the gift of faith and confidence. But when one exercises the gift of faith by stating a goal or solution, he cannot doubt. Doubt is the opposite of confidence or the opposite of faith. Jesus tied faith and confidence together, saying, if a man "shall not doubt in his heart, but shall believe those things which he saith shall come to pass; he shall have whatsoever he saith" (Mark 11:23).

4. *Recognize the human factor in exercising the gift of faith.* The gift of faith is not the same as the gift of miracles. In an evident miracle, God is the source and channel that produces a supernatural intervention or transcending of the natural laws of the universe. In the gift of faith, God works through the human instrument and limits himself to the human expression of faith.

Whereas God is the source of the Christian work, the human is the channel through which he works.

Earlier, the illustration of Paul's statement in relation to the shipwreck was noted as a possible exercise of the gift of faith. Paul said what should be done (remain in Crete, Acts 27:21). Then Paul said to remain with the ship (v. 31), and eat (v. 33). With the statement of faith and God's providential care, the people were responsible for certain duties. They ate, rowed, swam, and were generally responsible to carry out the deliverance provided by God.

In the area of church growth, the pastor may set attendance goals or make a statement of faith that he will establish a church. But the accomplishment of the results is also the responsibility of the leader. He must follow proven principles to accomplish his goal.

SUMMARY

The gift of faith is a special ability to see and understand what God can do in a certain project, to trust God to bless the work so that a project is accomplished and, on some occasions, to move God to intervene in the natural flow of circumstances so that problems are solved, goals are reached, and protection is given to those needing it.

Most of the qualities possessed by men relate to themselves or their relationship to others, such as love, joy, peace, or patience. But of all the qualities available to men, faith is that one asset that pleases God and moves God to intervene in the affairs of man in an unusual or unexpected way. And those who have the gift of faith seem to personify that ability to the greatest degree. "If ye have faith as a grain of mustard seed, ye shall say unto this mountain, Remove hence to yonder place; and it shall remove; and nothing shall be impossible unto you" (Matt. 17:20).

15
HOW TO APPLY
THE GIFT OF FAITH

This book has tried to show a correlation between faith and church growth: i.e., that the pastor who properly exercises faith will motivate his church to growth. If this thesis is true, then the opposite may also be operative—the leader who does not exercise faith will have little, if any, church growth. Out of this conclusion grow several practiced applications for church growth. These principles will guide those who desire more faith and those who desire church growth.

1. *Faith is one of the primary influences on church growth.* Whether the pastor believes that faith is caused/interventional, or faith is passive/instrumental, this study tends to conclude that those pastors with the strongest perception of their faith also have growing churches. This does not prove that faith and church growth have a cause-and-effect relationship. It could mean that pastors with the strongest perception of faith have other qualities that caused their church to grow, such as confidence, self-acceptance, goal-orientation, or some other trait that may be a by-product of faith. But the practical application is evi-

dent: those who want to grow should give attention to their faith.

2. *Those with growing churches also have growing faith.* Each of the Liberty men testified that his faith has grown since he started his church. At the same time, each of the churches were growing. This does not say that the pastors' growing faith caused their churches to grow, or vice versa. But there is a correlation between the two; Liberty men testified that their growing faith produced growing churches.

3. *The pastors of growing churches have the gift of faith.* Some of the "spiritual gifts" literature doubts the existence of a separate gift of faith. It says that all spiritual gifts become operative with general faith. But Liberty men testified they possessed or previously had the gift of faith. Some had questions about their gift and others did not emphasize their gift, but none doubted the existence of the gift of faith and its role in church growth.

4. *Pastors can grow their churches through the gift of faith and they can sharpen their spiritual gift of faith to be more effective.* This study concludes that (1) there is a gift of faith; (2) it is a capacity for Christian service; (3) it grows in its effectiveness; and (4) it can produce church growth.

5. *If pastors do not have the gift of faith, they can seek it.* This study has concluded that spiritual gifts are given to believers, perhaps when the Holy Spirit indwells them at salvation, and that the gift of the Holy Spirit provides the embryonic or latent capacities for service called spiritual gifts. Therefore, since the pastor has the germ seed of the gift of faith, he should seek to manifest it in his service.

6. *Pastors can increase the effectiveness of their spiritual gift.* This study has reflected the testimony of those who say their gift of faith has grown. There was no precise agreement as to how the gift of faith could

be developed, but there were some general steps. The effectiveness of the gift of faith can be increased by: (a) knowing and applying Scripture; (b) exercising the faith one already has; (c) praying; (d) trials; (e) fellowship or being influenced by those who already have the gift of faith; (f) learning from the past work of God in one's life; (g) being a clean vessel; (h) setting and accomplishing goals; (i) growing in Christian character; and (j) growing the gift of faith as the church grows.

7. *Church growth is realized as the pastor progresses from instrumental faith to interventional faith.* Church growth is influenced as pastors: (a) use faith as an *instrument* to accomplish the work of God; (b) use faith as *insight* or vision to see what God is doing or wants to do, then work to accomplish that dream; and (c) use faith to *intervene* against a crisis or to successfully meet a goal, whereby God gives victory over the problem and causes the church to grow.

8. *Those who use all three aspects of the gift of faith seem to have the greatest church growth.* No one can be certain whether the pastors interviewed were using all three aspects of the gift of faith to produce growth. We must rely on the testimony of those who say they have the gift of faith. Even then, the certainty of how they employed faith is not known. But those who began at (a) instrumental faith; then went on to (b) insight; and finally employed (c) interventional faith, seemed to accomplish the most. To bring another qualification into perspective, those who claim to have interventional faith may, in fact, misinterpret the circumstances concerning faith. Their church growth may come from some other motivation. Whether this perspective is true, the fact is that Liberty men perceive their gift of faith and relate their church growth to it.

9. *The gift of faith as an instrument can be used by the pastor to influence church growth.* The quality of faith

is measured by its source, which is Jesus Christ as revealed in Scripture. Faith is not measured by the subjective trust of the pastor. Therefore, any spiritual growth in an individual, or in a church, must come as the pastor uses faith as an instrument to build up individuals or the church. Then faith, like prayer, the Scriptures, or witnessing, is an instrument to effect spiritual growth in a broad range of areas. Instrumental faith will produce numerical growth, but probably not in a clear cause-and-effect relationship. When the pastor uses instrumental faith, the total spiritual quality of the church increases and numerical growth usually results, but not in every instance.

10. *The gift of faith as insight/vision can be used by the pastor to influence church growth.* Faith is the capacity to see what God is doing or wants done in an area; then the pastor can work to accomplish that goal. Vision or insight may include the ability to see the proper location to plant a church; the ability to see the principles that can work in an area; the ability to understand and apply doctrine to a group of people; or the ability to perceive the size and/or varied ministries of a potential church. Therefore, church growth begins with insight/vision, which becomes the foundation for meaningful labor. Hence, vision has a correlation to church growth.

11. *The gift of faith can intervene in crises that face a church or solve problems that hinder growth.* Varied interpretations of theology are involved in this principle. Some believe the day of signs and miracles is past; therefore, they probably would reject the view which implies that faith is the causal agent to motivate God to do the impossible. Others believe signs and miracles exist today; therefore, they probably accept the miraculous nature of faith. This study has concluded that interventional faith is located between the two positions. Granted, God controls his universe

through his laws, and the day of miraculous signs and revelations is past; but God obviously works today in an experiential way. The filling of the Spirit, answers to prayer, and the illumination of the Holy Spirit all testify to the present-day work of God in the world. These operate in the Christian's spiritual experience with implications for the physical world. Therefore, the gift of faith can have an experiential influence on the work of God. When the pastor says to the mountain, "Be thou removed, and be thou cast into the sea; and shall not doubt in his heart, but shall believe those things which he saith shall come to pass; he shall have whatsoever he saith" (Mark 11:23). This is interventional faith to solve crises and overcome barriers that keep a church from growing. Therefore, interventional faith can lead to church growth.

12. *Pastors do not have to express their faith in the same manner as other pastors to influence church growth.* It is obvious from this study that Liberty men do not all agree on how to express their faith. Yet all the Liberty men that were examined were growing in spite of their differences. One Liberty man said that faith was not getting a "handle on God," while others were seeking that special edge that faith would produce. Some might wonder how different expressions of faith could influence church growth. Remember, faith pleases God, "for he that cometh to God must believe that he is, and that he is a rewarder of them that diligently seek him" (Heb. 11:6). God is pleased by those who trust him for church growth; therefore, in spite of their varied expression, doctrinal beliefs, or other deviations, he rewards them according to their faith.

13. *The gift of faith can be stimulated in pastors by those who exercise their gift.* Most of the Liberty men testify that Jerry Falwell either taught them faith or motivated them to use their faith. Earlier, the author

called this the "hot poker" method of transferring the gift of faith from one person to another. Just as the hot coals heat the poker, so spiritual gifts are transferred/ stimulated by the person who exercises them (Rom. 1:11). Therefore, to apply this principle, the pastor who wants to grow in faith should expose himself to those with faith as they exercise it. This can be done through sermons, seminars, tapes, counseling, books, etc.

14. *Pastors should refine their unique expression of faith because it will not manifest itself exactly in them as it has in their teachers.* The obvious conclusion is that the students of Jerry Falwell do not generally agree with his expression of the gift of faith. Falwell, according to those who know him, seeks to exercise interventional faith, yet several of the Liberty students did not feel they could use interventional faith. However, their disagreement did not mean they felt Falwell was wrong. They felt faith could be expressed in different ways. Two students who once believed like Falwell have changed their position on the application of faith. This study does not attempt to draw a line between Falwell and his students, but to point out that even in a system perceived to be closed, students not only have the freedom to express their indigenous beliefs, but in fact to disagree. But even in their disagreement, the students credit Falwell with motivating them in faith for their ministry; and as a result, they constantly exercise their faith to cause their church to grow. For a practical application, pastors should realize that their faith may have a different expression from their spiritual "heroes," and that their members may express *their* faith differently. Therefore, everyone should work out his unique expressions of faith.

15. *Goal-setting can be a unique expression of the gift of faith.* Several Liberty men have learned to set and achieve goals as an expression of faith. Setting goals

will challenge the whole church to faith when the goal (a) has a biblical basis; (b) is scriptural in its motivation; (c) is achieved; and (d) glorifies God rather than the man or the church. In the practical area, goal-setting can relate to attendance, visitors, offering, conversions, obtaining property, or other tangible measures of achievement.

16. *Announcing or asking for victories over problems or solutions to crises can be an expression of the gift of faith.* There is a fine line between spiritual "pride of life" and announcing an answer to prayer before the answer is delivered. In one sense, the pastor must condition everything on the premise, "If the Lord will" (James 4:15). David Rhodenhizer was the most open about admitting missed goals. He said that on occasions he had a wrong perception of faith in setting goals, when in actuality the natural laws of church growth were broken. Therefore, he did not get what he set as a faith goal. Yet one failure did not discourage him from making other faith statements.

17. *There is a close correlation between the pastor's perception of the strength of his faith and the actual strength of his faith.* Some pastors wrongly emphasize their doubts or weak faith, thinking that a show of humility will strengthen their faith. Other pastors take the opposite stance, acting as if they have strong faith, thinking their strong attitude will strengthen their weak faith. Faith is not strengthened by "psyching up" oneself, nor "debasing oneself." Faith comes from Jesus Christ (Heb. 12:1, 2) through the Word of God (Rom. 10:17). In this study, the perception of faith was measured and compared among ten men. While the author assumes honesty in the responses he received, he is aware that the respondees may be honest but at the same time may be wrong in their judgment of their faith. Even taking the possibility of error into consideration, there still could be a correlation between faith

(which involves a perception of God) and a person's perception of his faith. Perhaps there is some credibility or reality in perception. Since God expects faith (which involves perception) and God expects each person to strengthen his faith (which involves correctly perceiving his faith if he is to strengthen it), then a correlation between faith and perception can be expected.

This principle becomes practical when the pastor (a) honestly accepts the inner perception he has of his faith; (b) honestly seeks to strengthen his faith; (c) does not become guilty for his lack of faith; and (d) exercises the faith he perceives he has for church growth. (If a pastor thinks he has faith, he should act on it.)

18. *Pastors who properly exercise their faith when they know they are in the geographical location where God wants them will have a better opportunity to grow.* The Liberty men all testified that God led them, by faith, to their location. They were so sure of his leading that most of them testified they probably would not have experienced the blessing of God as greatly in another location. When Liberty men measured the assessment of their faith in relation to location, those with the fastest growing churches scored the highest. Those with less growth scored lower in perception of faith and location. The author is not sure whether God (potentially) blesses them more in one location than another; or whether they have more confidence in one location, therefore their churches grow because of a confident leader. There is no question in the minds of Liberty men: they feel God will bless them more if they are in the correct location. In a practical way, pastors who are confident of God's leading them to their location will probably enjoy more growth than those who minister without confidence.

19. *Pastors who express their faith with allegiance*

to correct doctrine will influence church growth. The Liberty men testified that others who disagree with them in minor points of theology are still growing; but they all insisted that faith in the cardinal points of theology are necessary for the church to grow in a biblical sense. The Liberty men who made the strongest assessment of faith in doctrine had bigger growth than the average Liberty man who made a lower assessment of faith in doctrine. Hence, there is a correlation between faith in doctrine and church growth. This assessment did not attempt to determine the correctness of doctrine and church growth, nor did it attempt to determine the type (position or interpretation) of doctrine and church growth. This study only assessed the strength of a pastor's faith in relation to church growth. Those with the strongest perception of their faith had the fastest growth.

Some may say that faith was not measured, but there was only measurement of the pastor's sincerity. If this is true, then pastors with the most sincerity had the most growth. But the testimony of the Liberty men indicates that their faith in doctrine was a determination in the growth of their church.

20. *Pastors who express their faith by carrying out the objectives of the church as found in the Great Commission influence church growth.* The Liberty men who are growing said that the Great Commission is the objective of the church. Those who had the strongest assessment of faith to carry out the Great Commission had greater growth than the average Liberty graduate who had lesser growth and lower assessment of the strength of his faith to carry out the Great Commission.

Liberty men recognized that there were others who disagreed with their view of the objectives of the church. They recognized that pastors of other churches were growing even when they led their church from a different set of objectives. Basically, they rejoiced for any type of ministry or church growth that honored the Lord.

As a practical application, the pastor who attempts to implement the Great Commission may probably have church growth. The growth of the church will probably come with the following motives: (a) The pastor sincerely expresses his faith by accepting the Great Commission as the church's objectives. (b) The pastor obeys the Great Commission by reaching lost people, incorporating them into the church and teaching them the Scriptures. The church grows, regardless of the spiritual dynamics of faith, because natural laws of outreach and incorporation are followed. (c) Interventional faith will challenge and solve the crisis that prohibits evangelism or will set goals that motivate the pastor and/or congregation to achieve evangelistic results; hence, the church will grow.

21. *The pastor who expresses faith in the principles of church growth will influence growth.* Liberty men did not always agree with the principles of evangelism they had learned, but they were committed to the principles they were attempting to use in ministering to their church. The Liberty pastors of the fastest growing churches had a stronger assessment of faith in implementing their principles than did the average Liberty graduate who had less church growth and lower assessment of their faith in relation to church growth principles.

As a practical application, the pastor who would grow should implement the following suggestions: (a) He should exercise faith when he is involved in evangelistic outreach. Liberty men testified that God honored their faith because they obeyed him in using their evangelistic principles. (b) He should use those principles in which he has confidence (this is faith in

principles, because he believes they come from God).
(c) He should have a biblical foundation for his principles (because the Word of God will strengthen the
faith of a pastor) so he can minister in confidence.
(d) Faith in God is expressed in using principles that
are both biblical and number-oriented, which will
lead to church growth.

FINAL WORD

This study has concluded that the pastor with the
strongest assessment of his faith will influence
church growth when (1) his faith uses the Bible as
an instrument to provide individual and corporate
growth in spiritual areas; (2) his faith sees a vision
of what God wants to accomplish in the church, hence
clarifying objectives, making definite plans, and providing motivation as the basis for recruiting others to
assist in carrying out the dream; (3) his faith intervenes to solve crises, remove growth barriers, or successfully establish and achieve goals; (4) his faith
finds the divinely appointed geographical location so
that he can develop a confident ministry; (5) his faith
confidently communicates the doctrine that he knows
will be blessed by God; (6) his faith implements the
obvious results that are inherent when the objectives
of the Great Commission are carried out in the
church; (7) his faith sincerely applies the biblical
principles of evangelism so that people profess Christ
as Savior, fellowship with the church, and are taught
the Word of God. When the gift of faith is so exercised,
the church will grow, believers will be edified, and
God will be glorified.

APPENDIX I
Measuring Ten
Attitudes of Faith

We now attempt to measure what many think cannot be measured—the gift of faith. At one place, Jesus seemed to imply that either a person has faith, or he does not. When Jesus likened faith to a grain of mustard seed, he seemed to be comparing it to what those in that day considered one of the smallest perceptible objects in life. "If ye have faith as a grain of mustard seed, ye shall say unto this mountain, Remove hence to yonder place; and it shall remove" (Matt. 17:20). Apparently, this is a reference to the serving gift of faith, for Paul uses the same metaphor in relation to spiritual gifts: "And though I have the gift of prophecy, and ... all faith, so that I could remove mountains" (1 Cor. 13:2). Some might interpret this to mean all a person needs is faith, no matter how small, in order to move mountains. If small faith can move a mountain, why should it grow? Some might take another step and say that if small faith is all that is necessary, it does not need to grow, or it cannot grow.

But, since other spiritual gifts can grow, it is not unusual to expect the gift of faith to grow. Also, since Christ made the correlation between faith and a seed, and a seed can grow, perhaps he was implying that faith could grow. But to suggest a balance, perhaps faith in God remains constant, but the person grows. When the person steps out in faith, he strengthens himself for a future step of faith. Then it is not faith that grows, but the person who grows in his experience as he learns how to exercise his faith in God. The spiritual gift of faith retains the same capacity, but the person grows in his ability to apply his gift in Christian service.

This chapter attempts to examine the expression of faith in the life and ministry of ten church planters by analyzing each in his assessment of faith, then comparing it to the statistical measurements of his church. The ten are chosen because they were influenced by Dr. Jerry Falwell, pastor of Thomas Road Baptist Church, and they have used similar techniques and attitudes in building their churches.

There are many ways that Jerry Falwell has expressed the gift of faith: i.e., by setting attendance goals, financial goals, building projects, missionary projects, and expansion goals for the television ministry of the Old Time Gospel Hour. However, this study has chosen to examine the expression of faith in relation to church planting in the United States. On many occasions, Falwell stated a goal of planting 5,000 new churches in this country.[1] There is a general support among the employees at Liberty Baptist College for the institution's goals, and usually the goals are reached. However, not everyone accepts the possibility of reaching these goals. One faculty member presented a paper to a special committee studying the aims of ministerial preparation that indicated the goal of 5,000 new churches by A.D. 2000 was not possible.[2]

Between October 1973, when the first graduates left Liberty, and October 19, 1982, a total of 211 new churches were begun.[3] In 1982, the year this study was done, a total of 30 new churches were planted.[4]

Mathematically, the goal of 5,000 new churches by A.D. 2000 seems impossible if the present size of the college is considered and the present rate of church-planting continues. But this is where the gift of faith is reflective of the ability of God's man to see what can be accomplished (insight faith), and his trust in God to accomplish what is impossible (interventional faith). The goal of 5,000 new churches can be reached because the college will grow and will graduate an increasing number of church planters. Also, the multiplication of new churches by the existing church (apart from Liberty graduates) will cause spiraling growth. As an illustration, Al Henson (LBS, '81), pastor of Lighthouse Baptist Church, Nashville, Tennessee, has planted 15 churches that are not yet counted toward the goal of 5,000 churches.

In 1981, the authors organized the Liberty Baptist Fellowship for Church Planting, Inc. (LBF) to assist in carrying out the goal of planting 5,000 new churches.[5] The Liberty Baptist Fellowship for Church Planting, Inc., is an organization with a threefold purpose: (1) to motivate church planting; (2) to assist church planting with finances; and (3) to gather and disseminate information on church planting by Liberty graduates with a view to motivate the planting of new churches everywhere by all Christian organizations.[6]

The membership consists of: (a) graduates from Liberty Baptist Seminary, Liberty Bible Institute, and Liberty Baptist College; (b) former students—not graduates from the three institutions; (c) former staff members from Thomas Road Baptist Church, The Old Time Gospel Hour, or one of the Liberty Schools; (d) church planters helped financially by Thomas Road Baptist Church; (e) young men who were members of the church but not on staff, or a student at one of the schools; (f) church planters who have been influenced by Jerry Falwell and have a "Liberty-type" church.

A "Liberty type" church is characterized by the following seven points. (1) Super-aggressive evangelism, which means their purpose is to "capture their Jerusalem for Christ" by preaching, teaching, soulwinning, and discipling as many people as possible.

(2) Growing churches, *which is the biblical mandate and outcome of the ministry of these churches, so much so that they believe in large churches. (However, large is measured in relation to the "Jerusalem" in which they minister, so that a large church in one town may be measured by the 100s while in another town, it may be measured by the 1,000s.) (3)* Independent, *which means each church receives its authority from God and is responsible only to God. They are not, nor ever shall be, bound by tradition, denomination, or the vote of any fellowship, including Liberty Baptist Fellowship. (4)* Biblical separation, *which means they are committed to preach, teach, and practice both personal and corporate separation from sin. (5)* Fundamentalism, *which means that they are committed to believe in and aggressively defend the biblical fundamentals of the faith. (6)* Ecclesiastical separation; *they will have no fellowship with individuals, churches, or groups that deny the fundamentals of the faith. (7)* Two offices; *these churches recognize pastors and deacons (Phil. 1:1). The pastor is a ruling office, which means he is called, gifted for the office of leader of the flock (1 Tim. 5:17; Heb. 13:7, 17; 1 Tim. 3:4; 1 Pet. 5:1-4; 1 Thess. 5:12; 1 Cor. 16:16; Acts 20:28). The deacons are a serving office of the church, but the church congregation is the final authority in all matters.*

In September 1982, a survey was mailed to all 211 church planters on the mailing list of the LBF. A second mailing was sent in October. A total of 87 responses were received by October 15, 1982, for a 41 percent return. The data are drawn from similar type churches, hence there is a basis for correlation among the churches. By joining LBF, the church planters have indicated that both they and their churches are similar in polity and doctrine to the Liberty-type church. Whether they are "exactly" similar, or whether they have some similarities only because the church planter perceives himself and his church as a Liberty-type, is sufficient comparison to arrive at some tentative conclusions. A church planter would probably not join LBF unless he is in basic agreement with its objectives, polity, and doctrine, because of the stigma and criticism that Falwell has evoked by his position as President of Moral Majority Inc., or his visible stand on issues that are questionable to certain Christians.

The survey revealed that in 1982, the average church pastored by a Liberty graduate had an average attendance of 138 in Sunday school and 162 in the morning worship. There was an average of 33 baptisms per year in each church and an average membership of 151. The average Liberty church has a yearly income of $69,013, or a per capita income of $8.19 per attender each week.

PROFILE OF A CHURCH PLANTED BY A LIBERTY GRADUATE	
Average Sunday school attendance	132
Average church attendance	162
Average membership	151
Average yearly income	$69,013
Total reported income in 1982 of churches planted by Liberty men	$14,561,776
Per capita income	$8.19
Average number of baptisms per church	33
Total number of baptisms in 1982 in churches planted by Liberty men	7,137

The members of the Liberty Baptist Fellowship were surveyed to find the ten churches with the fastest growth rate over a decade (Decadal Growth Rate). Only churches that had been in existence for five years and had constructed or purchased a building were selected to determine the fastest growth. These churches had evidenced some maturity, had constructed a building, and had been in existence long enough for the pastor to face and solve some normal problems connected with growth. Also, most charts determine Decadal Growth Rate (DGR) based on church membership. However, the average Liberty man puts the most emphasis on attendance, not membership. Many churches did not have membership figures. Peter Wagner has indicated that there is an unusually high growth rate if the first two years of a church's existence is used to determine its rate of growth. At first, it was thought that these would be eliminated in formulating their rate of growth. But if the first two years were eliminated in the growth charts, there would be only three years to measure on growth charts, which is inadequate to diagnose or make observations regarding growth. Therefore, all five years are used to determine the rate of growth, but the reader should remember not to compare these rates with churches that have been in existence longer.

THE TEN FASTEST DECADAL GROWTH RATES AMONG LIBERTY GRADUATES	
Pastor and Church	Percentage
1. Al Henson, Lighthouse Baptist Church	9695
2. Rod Kidd, Heritage Baptist Church	5906
3. Steve Ray, Holy Mountain Baptist Church	4582
4. John Martelli, Wachusett Valley Baptist Church	3808
5. Marvin Wood, Harvest Baptist Church	3039
6. David Rhodenhizer, Calvary Road Baptist Church	2453
7. Kurt Strong, Freeport Baptist Church	1992
8. Ronnie Riggins, New Life Baptist Church	1128
9. Gary Byers, Fredericktowne Baptist Church	570
10. Bob Gehman, Baltimore County Baptist Church	123

MEASURING THE GIFT OF FAITH

Jerry Falwell and the pastors having the ten largest growth rates were asked to fill out a survey that assessed their faith on a scale of one to ten, from weak faith to strong faith. This survey asked them to measure their faith at the time they planted the church and again in the fall of 1982. Then the survey asked them to measure their faith on a scale of one to ten in relation to four areas: location, doctrine, church objectives, and principles.

THE ASSESSMENT OF FAITH BY CHURCH PLANTERS

	Faith at time of planting	Faith in 1982	Faith and location	Faith and doctrine	Faith and church objectives	Faith and principles
Falwell	5	8.1	10	9	8	7.5
Average of all Liberty men responding	8.1	8.1	6.7	6.3	6.6	6.0

ASSESSMENT OF FAITH BY CHURCH PLANTERS: TEN FASTEST DECADAL GROWTH RATES

	Faith at time of planting	Faith in 1982	Faith and location	Faith and doctrine	Faith and church objectives	Faith and principles
Henson	8	9	9	6.5	6	6.5
Kidd	5	9	9	7	9	7.5
Ray	10	10	9.5	8.5	8.5	7.5
Martelli	7	9	8.5	7.5	8	7.5
Wood	10	10	10	10	10	10
Rhodenhizer	10	10	8.5	7	9	7
Strong	8	9	8.5	8.5	9	7.5
Riggins	7	8	8.5	8	8.5	9
Byers	10	10	9	9	9	9
Gehman	10	10	9	9	8.5	8.5
Average of Ten Fastest DGR	8.7	9.3	8.9	8.2	8.8	8.1

The ten Liberty graduates differ in the perception of their faith and how they express their faith. The question does not deal with an actual or correct assessment of their faith, but how they perceived it at a point in time.

	CHURCH PLANTERS LISTED IN ORDER OF GROWTH	
Name	Strength of faith when church planted	Strength of faith now
a. Henson	8	9
b. Kidd	5	9
c. Ray	10	10
d. Martelli	7	9
e. Wood	10	10
f. Rhodenhizer	10	10
g. Strong	7	8
h. Riggins	8	9
i. Byers	10	10
j. Gehman	10	10

STRENGTH OF FAITH AT THE TIME OF PLANTING THE CHURCH

				1		2	2		5*
1	2	3	4	5	6	7	8	9	10
weak				average					strong

Represents number of church planters from 10 fastest DGRs

It is interesting that five church planters did not rank their faith "Strong/10" when they planted their churches, but all of them assessed their faith equal to, or stronger, in 1982. Also, note that three of the pastors with the fastest growth rate ranked their faith weaker than the average Liberty man when they planted the church, but in 1982 they were all stronger, or equal to, the average Liberty graduate. Apparently, they were growing in the perception of faith (either their growing church strengthened their faith, or the reverse happened).

STRENGTH OF FAITH IN FALL 1982									
							1	**4**	**5***
1	**2**	**3**	**4**	**5**	**6**	**7**	**8**	**9**	**10**
weak				average					strong

*Represents number of church planters
from 10 fastest DGRs*

After the assessment of the strength of the faith by the ten church planters was made on a scale of one to ten in relation to four factors—(a) location, (b) doctrinal statement, (c) expressed church objectives, and (d) the application of proper church planting principles—four quartiles were constructed to compare the results. Then the ten church planters were placed on the quartiles and compared with the average Liberty Baptist Fellowship church planter.

A. *A quartile comparison of faith and location.* The following quartile was constructed to determine a comparison of the assessed faith of the church planter to his location. The church planter was asked to assess the strength of his perception of God's leading him to the city where he ministered (horizontal). This was compared to the assessment of his faith (vertical). All Liberty church planters scored in the upper right-hand quartile.

There is a corrective factor in the questions. When the church planter was asked to assess the strength of his commitment to a geographical location, the author assumed the church planter would rank himself high in his commitment to a location because the environment at Liberty motivates a church planter to find a location for a church to which God is leading him, or to allow God to burden his heart for a city. For a Liberty man to affirm anything less than a high score, is to question his training. Therefore, the corrective question was asked, "If you had left this location to go elsewhere for ministry, how much could God bless your ministry in another place?" He was then asked to rank the question on a scale from one to ten. It was assumed if the Liberty man were committed to his present location, he would score low on another location. The result of the corrective answer was reversed on the scale and averaged with the first question to produce a composite or corrective score.

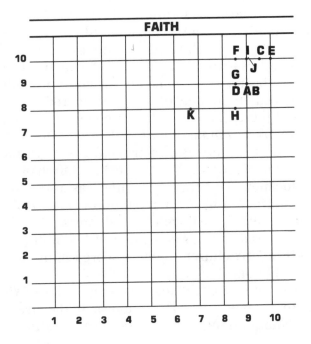

A.	Henson	9/9	G.	Strong	9/8.5
B.	Kidd	9/9	H.	Riggins	8/8.5
C.	Ray	10/9.5	I.	Byers	10/9
D.	Martelli	9/8.5	J.	Gehman	10/9
E.	Wood	10/10	K.	Average Liberty response	8/6.7
F.	Rhodenhizer	10/8.5			

10/10 strong faith—strong location. Note the obvious relationship of the ten Liberty men in the 10/10 quartile. Those who scored in the upper right-hand box would be expected to have a strong feeling of faith that God was directing them to the location where they are ministering. There are at least two possible conclusions for their success. If they knew they were in the correct geographical location, they would expect God to bless them in the church. On the other hand, if they felt strong faith in God, they would expect his direction to the correct location for a successful ministry. Only one church planter, Ronnie Riggins, had stronger faith identified with his location than with his personal faith. Also, he was the only one invited by someone to come to the location and begin the church.

Note the response of the average Liberty church planter. He was stronger in faith than in his commitment to the location, but his expressed commitment to both location and faith were weaker than the ten church planters with the fastest churches.

10/1 strong faith—weak location. Those who scored in this quartile would probably have a strong perception of their faith, but they are probably not completely convinced that the present location is the will of God. This person could be successful in his present location, or he could be successful in another place, because he has not tied faith to a location. His commitment to God is the primary consideration. Place is probably not a consideration unless he felt it was the wrong place. Then, a negative location would affect his faith; hence it would affect the success of his work.

1/10 strong location—weak faith. This person may have a strong commitment to a geographical location for many reasons. He may be committed to the area because of a burden to help needy people or the lack of a church in the area. Or, he may have lived in the area or originally come from there. Yet this same church planter may have weak faith for a number of reasons (see 1/1). In some cases, the church planter has faith that God will work in the area, perhaps not through his ministry but through someone else. In any case, the predictability of success is lower because the church planter has low belief/confidence that God will work in his ministry, even though he is in an area where he feels God would have him minister.

1/1 weak faith—weak location. Some may wonder how a church planter could ever end up in this situation. Sometimes a denomination has sent or assigned a man to a needy area, but the minister has no confidence that it is God's will for him to be there. As a result, he has little faith that God will use him there. Perhaps his low faith erodes any commitment he might have to the area. On the other hand, he may dislike the area or have some other negative feeling for the location that may erode his faith that God will use him in that place. Some may continue to minister in a 1/1 situation because it is a temporary assignment. Perhaps some continue to minister in a 1/1 situation because they wrongly interpret faith and yieldedness. They mistakenly think they are not to quit, they are to minister where situations are difficult, inhumane, or unlikely to produce success. Perhaps others are not successful because of their interpretation of the Scriptures, or they are unduly influenced by the anti-success attitudes of excessive humanism. In any case, some remain in a 1/1 location.

Summary. All Liberty men score themselves high in their assessment of faith and location. Those who have the highest DGR, score higher than the average Liberty graduate. Apparently, the ten Liberty men have strong faith that God led them to their location. Since the test measures only their perception of faith, the possibility exists that their faith is not the cause of church growth, but rather some other factor(s) caused the growth. This is not denying the possible growth of their faith. Their gift of faith could have grown as a result of their ministry. However, what is apparent is that these ten men testified that faith is the source of their church growth, so it must be accepted as the possible hypothesis.

B. *A quartile comparison of faith and doctrine.* The doctrinal quartile reflects the relationship between the assessment of the faith and commitment to doctrine of the church planter. The vertical line is the church planter's assessment of his faith when he planted the church. The horizontal line is the church planter's assessment of faith in relation to applying his doctrinal statement. (See graph on next page.)

As in the measurement of location, a corrective question was used to measure more accurately the church planter's assessment of doctrine. (See Appendix B for actual question.)

10/10 strong faith—strong doctrine. Those who scored in the upper right-hand quartile have a strong sense of personal faith in relation to the doctrinal foundation of their Christianity. The ten Liberty men scored in the 10/10 quartile, which is reflective of their strong faith and commitment to doctrine. They would conclude that their church has prospered because of their strong doctrine.

This study does not attempt to demonstrate that their doctrine is biblical or that it is the correct foun-

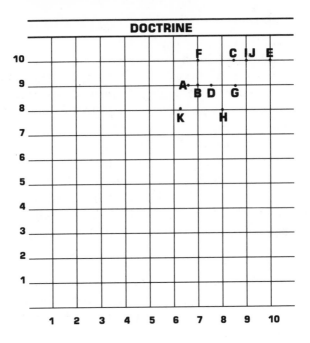

		Henson	9/6.5			Strong	9/8.5
A.	Henson	9/6.5		G.	Strong	9/8.5
B.	Kidd	9/7		H.	Riggins	8/8
C.	Ray	10/8.5		I.	Byers	10/9
D.	Martelli	9/7.5		J.	Gehman	10/9
E.	Wood	10/10		K.	Average Liberty response	8.1/6.3
F.	Rhodenhizer	10/7				

dation for church growth. The fact that others have had success in building a church, but were different from the Liberty men in doctrinal backgrounds, demonstrates some latitude in what doctrine is apparently blessed by God. This study examines the commitment the church planter makes to use doctrine as a foundation for his church. God blesses the exercise of faith by the church planter in the doctrine he assesses to be correct, not just the doctrinal content of a church planter. Also, an assumption is made (but not proven) that the average Liberty pastor holds similar doctrinal content as these ten church planters; but not all those pastors' churches have prospered to the same degree as those in this study.

The ten with the fastest growth rate scored higher than the average Liberty man, suggesting faith has a higher correlation to church growth than does doctrine. Also, nine of the Liberty men rated personal faith higher than commitment to doctrine. Riggins assessed faith and doctrine equally. Does this mean he has a more objective basis of faith than the others? This raises several questions that will not be examined in this study, but which should be answered. Why do Liberty men generally have a higher assessment of faith than of doctrine (one would assume that since faith comes from doctrine, doctrine would be assessed higher)? Do Liberty men tend toward mysticism because personal faith is assessed higher than doctrinal (objective) faith? Is there a connection between the higher assessment of personal faith and a tendency on their part to interventional faith?

10/1 strong faith—weak doctrine. This quartile reflects those who perceive their personal faith as strong, yet score themselves weak in relation to doctrine. This may be weak knowledge of doctrine; or a ministerial candidate may not be sure of his ability to apply it to people's lives. He may be committed to God but have some question of interpretation, not knowing if he is more Calvinist or more Arminian in persuasion. As a result, he may have scored his doctrinal commitment low. It is possible for such a minister to build a church if his sense of divine leadership to the location is high, or his confidence in church growth principles or church objectives can compensate for weak doctrine. Obviously, others have planted and built churches with low or little emphasis on doctrine.

1/10 strong doctrine—weak faith. This quartile represents those who have a strong commitment to doctrine, yet weak perception of their faith in God. The one with strong doctrinal commitment usually has more than a naive acceptance of God; he usually knows the person and works of God and his creation. Therefore, a 1/10 may not be weak in faith because he does not know about God. Perhaps he is not living consistently with his knowledge, hence he has a weak perception of faith. If he perceives faith as mystical or emotion-oriented, then he could perceive his faith as weak because he is an intellectual, not an emotion-oriented, person. In any case, his low faith would cause him to work without confidence or enthusiasm in his project. His ability to lead the church in growth would be affected. Those who score in the 1/10 could plant and build a church, but the predictability of success would be low and the rate of growth slow.

1/1 weak faith—weak doctrine. Those who score in this quartile would have the lowest predictability of outward growth in ministry. They would perceive their faith as weak, while also having a weak commitment to doctrine. Some may wonder if this person should be in full-time ministry. If he is not sure of his doctrine (the source of his message) or of his personal commitment to God (the source of his ministry), then perhaps he should examine his calling and qualifications for church planting or church growth.

Summary. The Liberty men score themselves high in their assessment of faith and doctrine. The ten whose churches have the highest growth rate score higher than the average Liberty man. Apparently they have stronger faith in relation to doctrine, which has a correlation to church growth. But the possibility exists that they assess their faith as stronger than it is in reality (perceptual). Also, their faith may not be the cause of growth; but, because their work has succeeded, their faith is the result of church growth. Faith could be the outgrowth, not the cause of their growth. But that is speculation; what is obvious is that they testify to a correlation of faith and doctrine as a source of their church growth. Perhaps the answer is not a single cause-and-effect relationship, but a correlation of many diffused factors.

C. *A quartile comparison of faith and objectives.* The following quartile determines the relationship between the assessment of a minister's faith and of his commitment to church objectives. The vertical line reflects the assessment of his faith, while the horizontal line reflects his assessment of his commitment to the church objectives taught at Liberty. Liberty church planters scored in the 10/10 quartile, strong faith—strong church objectives. A corrective question was used as in the previous chart (see Appendix B for the actual question).

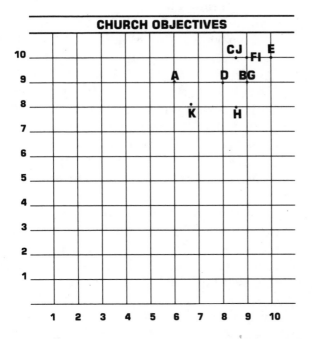

(See names on next page.)

A.	Henson	9/6	G.	Strong	9/9
B.	Kidd	9/9	H.	Riggins	8/8.5
C.	Ray	10/8.5	I.	Byers	10/9
D.	Martelli	9/8	J.	Gehman	10/8.5
E.	Wood	10/10	K.	Average Liberty response	8.1/6.6
F.	Rhodenhizer	10/9			

10/10 strong faith—strong objectives. Those who score in this quartile have a strong sense of faith and a strong commitment to the objectives of the church. The ten Liberty graduates with the highest DGR all scored in this quartile. Inasmuch as a clear perception of objectives is usually considered a basic criterion that leads to success in most projects, a church planter with clear objectives has a greater likelihood of success than one whose objectives are not clear, or who is not committed to his objectives. Liberty men are generally committed to the church objectives learned at Liberty: i.e., the Great Commission is the purpose of church planting and church growth.

The question concerning church objectives does not involve whether they are biblically correct or pragmatically workable. The question involves an assessment of the strength of the church planter to his church objectives. As in the other measurements, those who have a differing set of church objectives have demonstrated that they can plant and build a local church.[7]

The position of Liberty's doctrinal statement and the constitution of LBF is that the Great Commission is the articulated objective of the church. Liberty men are exhorted to: (1) win souls, (2) baptize converts, and (3) teach the Word of God. There are other articulated church objectives at Liberty, but these objectives are the ones which are prized by LBF, because statistics are gathered and distributed among the church plant-

ers regarding these areas. Hence, continual reinforce-
ment of these objectives to the present student body
and to those who are pastoring Liberty churches has
contributed to their success.

10/1 strong faith—weak objectives. Not all Liberty
graduates take Baptist churches; some end up in
other denominations. Some who take churches that
are non-Baptist in name carry out the Liberty objectives and make them Liberty-type churches. Others
take churches with objectives that are different from
those taught at Liberty. These were not measured
because there is no list available outside of the LBF
mailing list.

The commitment of the faith of any church planter,
no matter what his orientation, would make some
success in church growth predictable, even if he had
weak commitment to objectives. Surely many who
have been committed to God have applied the Bible
to their parishioners, resulting in God's blessing on
the church. Some of these were not clear in church
goals, nor were they committed to church growth.
But their commitment to "preach the Word" (2 Tim.
4:2) caused the church to prosper. However, it is the
author's contention that if such a person understood
church objectives and was committed to apply them
to his church, he probably would have enjoyed
greater blessings of God than he now enjoys.

1/10 weak faith—strong objectives. Obviously, those
who are not committed to their project (by ignorance
or by not being committed to the goals) and those
who personally do not express their faith in God for
their church (interpreted to mean no strength of faith
in God regarding church planting), will probably not
be able to build a growing church. There may be
social conditions in which a laissez-faire leader is
needed to pastor a group with low growth expectation
and weak direction. A 1/10 pastor may do well in such

a situation; and, if social conditions are right, the group may prosper. But the predictability of growth would be low.

1/1 weak faith—weak objectives. Those who score in this quartile would have a low predictability of success in church growth. They would perceive their faith as weak, while having a weak commitment to the objectives of the church. They may be weak in objectives because (1) they are ignorant of church objectives; (2) they believe the Bible teaches a strong commitment to individual objectives or parachurch objectives, rather than local church objectives; or (3) they have knowledge of church objectives, but for some personal reason they are not committed to them.

Summary. The Liberty men score themselves high in their assessment of faith as related to church objectives. The ten highest DGR score higher than the average Liberty pastor. Apparently, the strength of their faith in God as reflected in their church objectives is a factor in their growth. In view of the three types of faith, this section seems to be instrumental in nature. As in the last section, the Liberty men (except Riggins) rated their faith higher than church objectives. When church objectives are rated higher than faith, it would imply that faith had been instrumental (using faith as a tool for growth). But faith is ranked higher by Liberty men, suggesting an interventional approach to faith in church ministry and growth.

Also, the possibility exists that these men perceived their faith as stronger than it is in reality. If faith were ranked lower, then the instrumental conclusion could be suggested. But these men all testified to a strong correlation between faith and church objectives, suggesting faith is one hypothesis that leads to church growth.

D. *A quartile comparison of faith and principles.*

The following quartile measures the relationship between the assessment of faith by the church planter and his commitment to the principles and practices he applies in church growth. The vertical line is the church planter's assessment of his faith. The horizontal line is his assessment of his commitment to principles. A corrective question was used to determine the church planter's belief that God was blessing the principles used in his church, as opposed to his blessing different principles found in other growing churches (see Appendix B for the actual question).

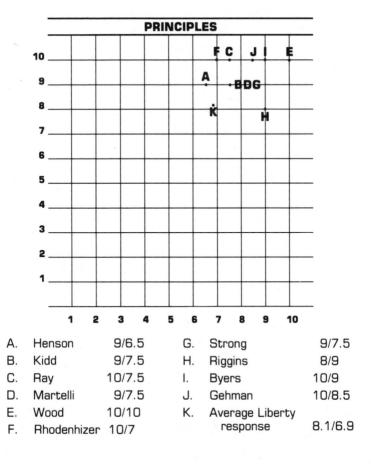

A. Henson	9/6.5	
B. Kidd	9/7.5	
C. Ray	10/7.5	
D. Martelli	9/7.5	
E. Wood	10/10	
F. Rhodenhizer	10/7	

G. Strong	9/7.5	
H. Riggins	8/9	
I. Byers	10/9	
J. Gehman	10/8.5	
K. Average Liberty response	8.1/6.9	

10/10 strong faith—strong principles. Those who scored in this quartile have a strong sense of faith and a strong commitment to church growth principles. There are at least two possible conclusions for their growth: first, their growth is the result of interventional faith; or, second, their growth is the result of the application of church planting and church growth principles. (The priority of the Word of God in the principles makes this second option instrumental faith.) The ten Liberty men scored in this quartile. Note, both groups (the ten church planters with the highest DGR [except Riggins] and the average Liberty man) scored themselves stronger in faith than in principles. Even though their assessment of principles is high (8.1), it is lower in comparison to the assessment of location (8.9), doctrine (8.2), and church objectives (8.8). Therefore, the Liberty men felt the correct principles to build a church were important, but not as important as other factors. Also, the interviews revealed that several Liberty men were no longer committed to saturation evangelism as a means of church growth.

10/1 strong faith—weak principles. Those who score in this quartile are strong in their assessment of faith, but weak in their commitment to principles. Those who rate themselves as weak may do so because of (1) ignorance of church principles, (2) no confidence that they are inducted from Scripture, or (3) lack of commitment to church growth principles for some personal reason. Such a minister could be successful in church growth, depending on the choice of principles he used (without being committed to them), or he could exercise his faith so that God intervenes to cause the church to grow.

10/1 strong principles—weak faith. The minister scoring in this quartile would assess his faith weak, but have a strong commitment to the principle he is employing. The correlation of church growth principles to the Bible is not the issue, for obviously more than one set of principles is used in church growth. The minister's assessment of these principles is the factor that is being measured. In certain circumstances, the success of a church can be predictable, based on the application of principles that are adaptable to the social context. However, faith (the intervention by God in marginal or adverse circumstances to build a church) will be a small factor in the 1/10 quartile.

1/1 weak faith—weak principles. Some might ask if a person could score in this quartile and remain in the ministry. Actually, there are probably a large number of ministers who assess themselves low in faith and low in commitment to church growth principles. There are several causes for a minister scoring in a 1/1 quartile: (1) he may be discouraged because of personal reasons, hence he exercises little faith in his ministry; (2) he has failed in some or many church ministry projects; (3) he does not minister from principles; (4) he is not committed to the principles he understands; (5) he has accepted the position that there are no principles of church growth taught in Scripture; or (6) he is ignorant of church growth principles.

Summary. The Liberty men score themselves high in their assessment of faith and church growth principles. The ten church planters with the highest DGRs assess themselves higher (8.1) than the average Liberty pastor (6.9). Apparently the correlation of faith with church growth principles is a factor that influences church growth. Inasmuch as the ten church planters scored faith higher than their commitment to principles (except Riggins), this would seem to imply that faith is an intervention factor to cause churches to grow. If they had rated principles stronger, then it might be implied that principles were the primary cause of growth, and faith the tool to apply the principles (instrumental faith).

The Liberty men scored lowest on principles in a comparison of the four factors of (1) location, (2) doctrine, (3) church objectives, and (4) principles. The average observer might have assumed the unique principles of saturation evangelism (as communicated in books, tapes, and conferences) to be the strongest scored by Liberty men. However, some graduates have conscientiously applied saturation evangelism and their church has not grown. Also, Jerry Falwell said that the heyday of saturation evangelism is past (the principle remains, but vast public acceptance is gone).[8] He explained that saturation evangelism was extremely successful when "cheap money" was available, but has been limited by inflation. He sees a problem with saturation evangelism because of the rising cost of advertising, Sunday school bus operation, building costs, salaries for expansion, and the prohibitive cost of purchasing time on television, radio, and other media. Falwell admonished his graduates to get "back to basics," which involves visitation, preaching, teaching, and soul-winning.

Some might argue that this measurement is only perceived—i.e., the Liberty men are building churches, but some other factor is the causal agent. This may be worth some consideration; however, the combined testimony cannot be ignored. These men perceive that their faith and their principles have caused churches to grow (even though this is lowest of four areas, it still is in the 10/10 quartile). Hence, the correlation of faith and principles is a hypothesis for church growth.

SUMMARY AND CONCLUSION

The most apparent observation is that those surveyed testified that they perceived their faith as stronger now than when they planted their church. The largest growth is reflected in Falwell, who went from 5 to 8. If this reflects a real rate of growth in faith (not just perception of growth), it proves that faith can grow. The total response to the survey indicates that they perceived that their faith had grown; and whether it grew or not, their stronger perception has a correlation to church growth. Whether their faith causes church growth or is the result of church growth, the perception of growth in faith seems to correlate to growth in the church.

APPENDIX II
Statistics of the
Ten Liberty Churches
With the Fastest DGR

TEN FASTEST GROWING CHURCHES—LIBERTY BAPTIST FELLOWSHIP

		Lighthouse Baptist Church Nashville, Tennessee	Heritage Baptist Church Lynchburg, Virginia	Holy Mountain Baptist Church Kingsport, Tennessee	Wachusett Valley Baptist Church Holden, Mass.	Harvest Baptist Church Charleston, So. Carolina	Calvary Road Baptist Church Alexandria, Virginia	Freeport Baptist Church Freeport, Illinois	New Life Baptist Church New Cumberland, Penn.	Fredericktowne Baptist Church Frederick, Maryland	Baltimore County Baptist Church Reistertown, Md.
Pastor		A. Henson	Rod Kidd	Steve Ray	John Martelli	Marvin Wood	David Rhodenhizer	Kurt Strong	Ronnie Riggins	Gary Byers	Bob Gehman
Average Sunday School Attendance	82		250	687	80	320	660	80	289	144	160
	81		190	463	90	234	437	65	343	117	145
	80		150	356	25	200	369	60	389	81	130
	79		85	310	20	110	314	50	228	106	135
	78		60	244	8	93	76	30	190	116	120
	77		35	116		58			143	117	100
	76					39			75	106	100
	75								23	100	100
Average Church Attendance	82		310	764	115	435	826	135	301	230	190
	81		250	573	160	318	574	85	356	151	178
	80		180	456	60	307	469	80	320	109	150
	79		110	390	35	140	392	70	246	121	164
	78		75	289	15	106	88	40	211	110	133
	77		40	142		90			177		125
	76					55			112		100
	75								52		100

Total Worth of Property & Buildings	$700,000	$350,000	$500,000	$275,000	$3,000,000	$400,000-$500,000	$350,000	$500,000	$460,000	
Church Began	Feb. '75	April '74	Dec. '75	June '78	Oct. '77	Aug. '76	Sept. '78	June '76	July '77	Jan. '78
Decadal Growth Rate	123%	570%	1128%	1992%	2453%	3039%	3808%	4582%	5906%	9695%
Membership 82	87	276	47	135	792	482	162	597	325	
81	n/a	218	70	97	n/a	360	173	465	225	
80	67	182	76	66	n/a	276	84	341	160	
79	63	157	61	49	n/a	145	36	280	90	
78	n/a	133	48	32	n/a	123	15	153	57	
77	40	84	76		n/a	100		132	37	
76	30	75	85		n/a	60				
75	26	36			n/a					
Baptisms 82	22	32	42	75	103	92	15	142	36	
81	31	13	90	13	88	100	19	89	30	
80	14	3	108	13	104		25	80	18	
79	24	4	76	13	101		26	84	9	
78	9	27	45	14	51			52	15	
77	22	22	109					46	9	
76	12	10	61							
75	14	45								
Income 82	$122,747	$ 81,761	$134,211	$64,454	$460,000	$178,795	$57,206	$264,000	$157,926	
81	108,000	104,726	160,193	64,437	367,419	203,665	52,097	203,000	144,279	
80	75,386	66,000	127,137	52,817	261,459	147,978	31,200	184,000	94,250	
79	63,924	63,745	99,251	50,393	n/a	99,485	20,800	102,000	182,295	
78	43,532	61,288	84,639	38,352	40,000	77,067	11,700	84,000	53,519	
77	28,979	65,975	64,183			41,990		64,000	33,224	
76	22,370		36,529			20,000			4,229	
75	14,148	33,647	1,480							

APPENDIX III
Questionnaire

TO BE ANSWERED ONLY BY THOSE
WHO PLANTED CHURCHES

1. *How would you interpret the strength of your faith at the time of planting this church?*

   1   2   3   4   5   6   7   8   9   10
   little   average   strong

2. *How would you rank your faith today?*

   1   2   3   4   5   6   7   8   9   10
   little   average   strong

3. *When God led you to plant this church, how strong was your commitment to your present city?*

   1   2   3   4   5   6   7   8   9   10
   little   average   strong

4. *If you had left this location to go elsewhere for ministry, how much could God bless your ministry in another place?*

   1   2   3   4   5   6   7   8   9   10
   little   average   strong

5. *How much of your church growth is the result of your commitment to a correct interpretation of doctrine?*

   1   2   3   4   5   6   7   8   9   10
   little   average   strong

6. *Some are experiencing church growth, yet differ with you in doctrine; how much of their growth do you attribute to the blessing of God?*

   1   2   3   4.   5   6   7   8   9   10
   little   average   strong

7. *How much of your church growth do you attribute to having correct church purpose?*

   1   2   3   4   5   6   7   8   9   10
   little   average   strong

8. *Some churches that disagree with your understanding of the priorities of the church are growing. How much of their growth do you attribute to the blessing of God?*

   1   2   3   4   5   6   7   8   9   10
   little   average   strong

9. *How much of your church growth is the result of applying biblical principles and practices?*

   1   2   3   4   5   6   7   8   9   10
   little   average   strong

10. *Some churches that disagree with your interpretation of biblical principles and practices are growing. How much of their growth do you attribute to the blessing of God?*

   1   2   3   4   5   6   7   8   9   10
   little   average   strong

APPENDIX IV
Interview Questions for an Analysis of the Gift of Faith in Church Growth

1. *What were the major steps of faith that resulted in the planting of this church?*

2. *Which was the biggest step of faith?*

3. *What was the source that strengthened your faith to plant this church?*

4. *What sources have caused your faith to grow since you have pastored this church?*

5. *Give some indications of the strength of your faith when God led you to plant this church.*

6. *What evidence did you have at the time that God would bless this church?*

7. *What would have happened to your faith if God had not caused this church to grow in this location?*

8. *What was the biggest financial step of faith you took that led to the expansion of this church?*

9. *Do you see any relationship between correct doctrine, faith, and church growth? What is it?*

10. *Can a person have strong faith and interpret Scripture differently from you?*

11. *Do you see any relationship between a correct understanding of the purpose of the church, faith, and church growth? What is it?*

12. *What is the purpose of the church?*

13. *What is the relationship between a correct application of biblical principles, faith, and church growth?*

14. *Do you believe there is a gift of faith that results in church growth?*

15. *If yes, is the gift of faith that results in church growth inborn, or can this gift be acquired and grow in its effectiveness?*

16. *Do you believe that anyone who is called of God can plant and grow a church if he exercises the same faith that you have followed?*

17. *Is your faith acquired or is it a sovereign gift of God? Why?*

18. *How can a pastor grow his faith so that it will be more effective in church growth?*

ENDNOTES

INTRODUCTION

[1]Elmer Towns, *The Ten Largest Sunday Schools* (Grand Rapids: Baker Book House, 1969); Elmer Towns, "The Seventy-five Largest Sunday Schools in America," *Christian Life* (August 1970):15.

[2]A description of the growth of Thomas Road Baptist Church and the results of faith are noted, but not analyzed in Elmer Towns and Jerry Falwell, *Church Aflame* (Nashville: Impact Books, 1971); Elmer Towns and Jerry Falwell, *Capturing a Town for Christ* (Old Tappan, N.J.: Fleming H. Revell Company, 1973).

[3]C. Peter Wagner, *Your Spiritual Gifts Can Help Your Church Grow* (Glendale, Cal.: Regal Books, 1979), p. 159.

CHAPTER 1

[1]Elmer Towns, *Say-It-Faith* (Wheaton, Ill.: Tyndale House, 1983). This book examines the relationship of doctrinal faith, saving faith, and serving faith.

[2]Towns and Falwell, *Church Aflame*, p. 43ff. The chapter is an exposition of the Great Commission, applying it to church objectives.

[3]One of the characteristics of fundamentalists is "literal obedience to primitive church ideas" summarized from Ernest Troeltsch, *The Social Teachings of the Christian Church*, trans. by Olive Wyan (London: George Allen and Unwin, 1931), 2 vols. The author equates fundamentalists (Falwell's position) and sects in *America's Fastest Growing Churches* (Nashville: Impact Books, 1972), pp. 156-168.

[4]Towns and Falwell, *Church Aflame*, pp. 70-96. Two chapters explain the principles of saturation evangelism. At times, Falwell interchanges the term *super-aggressive* (referring more to enthusiasm and zeal) with the term *saturation* (referring to principles).

CHAPTER 12

[1]John F. Walvoord, *The Holy Spirit* (Wheaton, Ill.: Van Kampen Press, 1954), p. 164.

[2]Walter Bauer, *A Greek-English Lexicon of the New Testament,* trans. by William F. Arndt and F. Wilbur Gingrick (Chicago: The University of Chicago Press, 1957), s.v., *charisma.*

[3]Joseph Henry Thayer, *A Greek-English Lexicon of the New Testament* translated, revised, and enlarged (New York: American Book Co., 1889), s.v., *charisma;* Colin Brown, *The New International Dictionary of New Testament Theology,* 3 vols. (Exeter, U.K.: The Paternoster Press, Ltd., 1978), s.v., *diakonia.*

[4]Ibid., s.v., *energeema.*

[5]Bauer, *A Greek-English Lexicon of the New Testament,* s.v., *phaneroo.*

[6]John R. W. Stott, *Baptism and Fullness* (Downers Grove, Ill.: InterVarsity Press, 1964), p. 87.

[7]Howard A. Snyder, *The Problem of Wine Skins* (Downers Grove, Ill.: InterVarsity Press, 1976), p. 132.

CHAPTER 13

[1]Gene A. Getz, *Sharpening the Focus of the Church* (Chicago: Moody Press, 1974), p. 127.

[2]Ibid., p. 127.

[3]Leslie B. Flynn, *Nineteen Gifts of the Spirit* (Wheaton, Ill.: Victor Books, 1974), p. 21.

[4]Albert Barnes, *Notes on the New Testament,* Matthew-Mark (Grand Rapids, Mich.: Baker Book House, 1949), p. 267.

[5]Charles C. Ryrie, *Biblical Theology of the New Testament* (Chicago: Moody Press, 1959), p. 196. In this volume, Ryrie implies that every Christian has a gift. As such each Christian has one gift. However, when the author took the course in Pauline Theology from Dr. Ryrie at Dallas Theological Seminary in 1956, Ryrie maintained that every Christian had the gifts of serving, giving, and encouraging.

[6]Flynn, *Nineteen Gifts of the Spirit*, p. 22.

[7]Robert Schuller, *Your Church Has Real Possibilities* (Glendale, Cal.: Regal Books, 1974). Schuller has popularized the term "possibility thinking," suggesting that one take a positive approach to ministry. He does not base his positive thinking on the gift of faith. Schuller feels if one "finds a need and fills it," a person's ministry will find receptivity, hence will be successful. Also, Schuller teaches that a person should use up-to-date methods of organization, marketing, and outreach. All of this, if done with faith in God, will prosper a church. As such, Schuller does not believe in the interventional, but the instrumental, approach to the gift of faith.

[8]Towns and Falwell, *Church Aflame,* chapter 5. The phrase "hot poker" is also used in several articles on church growth by the author and is his unique term to indicate how spiritual gifts are communicated on the human level.

[9]Ryrie, *Biblical Theology of the New Testament,* p. 196.

[10]Albert Barnes, *Notes on the New Testament,* 1 Corinthians (Grand Rapids, Mich.: Baker Book House, 1949), p. 267.

[11]Donald Gee, *Concerning Spiritual Gifts* (Springfield, Mo.: Gospel Publishing House, 1972), p. 42.

[12]John of St. Thomas, *The Gift of the Holy Spirit* (London: Sheed and Ward, 1951), p. 243.

[13]Ibid.

[14]Ibid.

[15]Ibid.

[16]Ibid.

[17]Harold Horton, *The Gifts of the Spirit* (Nottingham, England: Assembly of God Publishing House, 1934), p. 131.

[18]Flynn, *Nineteen Gifts of the Spirit,* p. 24.

[19]Ibid.

[20]Elmer Towns, *The Successful Sunday School and Teachers Guidebook* (Carol Stream, Ill.: Creation House, 1980), pp. 177, 178.

[21]Flynn, *Nineteen Gifts of the Spirit,* p. 24.

[22]Ibid.

[23]Ibid., p. 25.

[24]Ryrie, *Biblical Theology of the New Testament,* p. 196.

[25]Flynn, *Nineteen Gifts of the Spirit,* p. 24.

[26]Ibid., p. 25.

[27]Ibid.

[28]The author had designated six expressions of faith in the devotional book *Say-It-Faith* (Wheaton, Ill.: Tyndale House Publishers, 1983): (1) doctrinal faith, (2) saving faith, (3) justifying (imputed) faith, (4) indwelling faith, (5) daily faith, and (6) the gift of faith. A chapter is given to explain the meaning and use of each expression of faith.

[29]Kenneth Cain Kinghorn, *Gifts of the Spirit* (Nashville: Abingdon Press, 1976), p. 65.

[30]Kurt E. Koch, *Charismatic Gifts* (Montreal: The Association for Christian Evangelicals, 1975), pp. 90, 91.

[31]Howard Carter, *Spiritual Gifts and Their Operation* (Springfield, Mo.: Gospel Publishing House, 1968), p. 37.

[32]B. E. Underwood, *The Gifts of the Spirit* (Franklin Springs, Georgia: Advocate Press, 1967), p. 31.

[33]Gee, *Concerning Spiritual Gifts,* p. 42.

[34]Flynn, *Nineteen Gifts of the Spirit,* p. 140.

[35]Gee, *Concerning Spiritual Gifts,* p. 43.

[36]*The Living Bible* (Wheaton, Ill.: Tyndale House Publishers, 1971), p. 924.

[37]Underwood, *The Gifts of the Spirit,* p. 30.

[38]Koch, *Charismatic Gifts,* p. 91.

[39]John MacArthur, Jr., *The Church, The Body of Christ* (Grand Rapids, Mich.: Zondervan Publishing House, 1973), p. 144.

[40]Harold Friesen, "A Model for a Church in Ministry by Employing Spiritual Gifts Resulting in Spiritual and Numerical Growth" (D.Min. dissertation, Fuller Theological Seminary, 1979), p. 138.

CHAPTER 14

[1]Carter, *Spiritual Gifts and Their Operation,* p. 37.

[2]Ibid., p. 42.

[3]St. Thomas, *The Gifts of the Holy Spirit,* p. 243.

[4]C. Peter Wagner, *Your Spiritual Gifts Can Help Your Church Grow* (Glendale, Cal.: Regal Books, 1979), p. 158.

[5]Kinghorn, *Gifts of the Spirit,* p. 65.

[6]Flynn, *Nineteen Gifts of the Spirit,* p. 141.

[7]Wagner, *Your Spiritual Gifts Can Help Your Church Grow,* p. 159.

[8]Towns, *The Ten Largest Sunday Schools.* The author made this observation in chapter 13 after interviewing the pastors who were the leaders of the largest Sunday schools in America.

[9]Towns and Falwell, *Church Aflame,* pp. 44, 45.

[10]Gee, *Concerning Spiritual Gifts,* p. 43.

[11]Ibid.

[12]Underwood, *The Gifts of the Spirit,* p. 31.

[13]Horton, *The Gifts of the Spirit,* p. 31.

[14]Ibid., p. 131.

[15]The two interviews are found in two books by Elmer Towns, John Vaughan, and David Seifert, *The Complete Book of Church Growth* (Wheaton, Ill.: Tyndale House Publishers, 1981). This book reports that the Full Gospel Church had the largest membership in the world in 1981. *The World's Largest Sunday School* (Nashville: Thomas Nelson, Inc., 1974) reports First Baptist Church had the largest Sunday school in the world in 1974.

[16]George Barker Stevens, *The Theology of the New Testament* (Edinburgh: T. & T. Clark, 1899), p. 515.

[17]Ibid., p. 518.

[18]This thesis has not dealt with the unbelief of Christians, which apparently causes the disuse of faith. See Elmer Towns, *Say-It-Faith*, seven cassette C-60 tapes (Wheaton, Ill.: Domain Communication Ltd., 1982). Tape two, *The Pathologies of Faith*, deals with the six New Testament words that are ranked in various steps of unbelief. (1) *Vain faith*, 1 Corinthians 15:14-17, faith in the wrong doctrine. (2) *Dead faith*, James 2:19, 20, faith in orthodox doctrine without personal belief in Christ. These expressions of faith will not save a person. The next four refer to believers. (3) *Unbelief, epistis*, Mark 16:11-14; John 21, believers in Christ who will not accept his work. (4) *Little faith, oligopistis*, Mark 7:26, faith and unbelief mixed. (5) *Weak faith*, Romans 14:1, believers who have a legalistic expression of faith. (6) *Strong faith*, Romans 4:20, faith in the promise of God.

APPENDIX I

[1]Jerry Falwell, "We Will Plant 5,000 Churches," *Liberty Journal* 1 (September 1981):1.

[2]Woodrow Kroll, Former Chairman, Division of Religion, Unpublished study, paper presented to the Presidential Cabinet, "The Future of Graduate Work at Liberty."

[3]Second Annual Report, Liberty Baptist Fellowship, Lynchburg, Va., October 19, 1982.

[4]"Church Update," *Fundamentalist Journal* (Lynchburg, Va., February 1983).

[5]Editorial, "Who Is Liberty Baptist Fellowship?" *Liberty Journal* 1 (September 1981):2.

[6]Ibid., "New Fellowship Will Plant Churches," p. 1.

[7]Towns, Vaughan, and Seifert, *The Complete Book of Church Growth*, p. 89. This chart compares seven philosophies of church

growth. To some extent, there are different priorities and expressions of church growth objectives in each area. Yet there is numerical growth represented in each of the seven philosophies.

[8]Chapel message (April 1982) to ministerial students. Falwell has not committed this statement or explanation to print.

BIBLIOGRAPHY

BOOKS

Bresson, Bernard L. *Studies in Ecstasy.* N.Y.: Vantage, 1966.

Bridge, Donald. *Spiritual Gifts and Their Operation.* Springfield, Mo.: Gospel Publishing House, 1968.

Brown, Colin., gen. ed. *The New International Dictionary of New Testament Theology.* 3. vols. Exeter, U.K.: The Paternoster Press, Ltd., 1978. Vol. 3: *diakoneu,* by K. Hess.

Carter, Howard. *Spiritual Gifts and Their Operation.* Springfield, Mo.: Gospel Publishing House, 1968.

Cousins, Norman. *Human Options.* N.Y.: W.W. Norton and Company, 1981.

Flynn, Leslie B. *Nineteen Gifts of the Spirit.* Wheaton, Ill.: Victor Books, 1975.

Fowler, James W. *Stages of Faith.* San Francisco: Harper & Row, 1981.

Gee, Donald. *Concerning Spiritual Gifts.* Springfield, Mo.: Gospel Publishing House, 1972.

Guiness, Os. *In Two Minds: The Dilemma of Doubt and How to Solve It.* Downers Grove, Ill.: InterVarsity Press, 1976.

Hoge, Dean R., and Roozen, David A., eds. *Understanding Church Growth and Decline 1950-1978.* Princeton, N.J.: The Pilgrim Press, 1979.

Horton, Harold. *The Gifts of the Spirit.* Nottingham, England: Assembly of God Publishing House, 1934.

John of St. Thomas. *The Gifts of the Holy Spirit.* London: Sheed and Ward, 1951.

Judisch, Douglas. *An Evaluation of Claims to the Charismatic Gifts.* Grand Rapids, Mich.: Baker Book House, 1978.

Kelley, Dean M. *Why Conservative Churches Are Growing.* San Francisco: Harper & Row, 1977 (rev. ed.).

Kinghorn, Kenneth Cain. *Gifts of the Spirit.* Nashville: Abingdon Press, 1976.

Koch, Kurt E. *Charismatic Gifts.* Montreal: The Association for Christian Evangelists, 1975.

MacArthur, John, Jr. *The Church, The Body of Christ.* Grand Rapids, Mich.: Zondervan Publishing House, 1973.

MacGorman, Jack W. *The Gifts of the Spirit.* Nashville: Broadman Press, 1979.

McGavran, Donald and Hunter, George G. III. *Church Growth: Strategies at Work.* Nashville: Abingdon Press, 1980.

Ryrie, Charles C. *Biblical Theology of the New Testament.* Chicago: Moody Press, 1959.

Sanders, John Oswald. *The Holy Spirit and His Gifts.* Grand Rapids, Mich.: Zondervan Publishing House, 1970.

Snyder, Howard A. *The Problem of Wine Skins*. Downers Grove, Ill.: InterVarsity Press, 1976.

Stevens, George Barker. *The Theology of the New Testament*. Edinburgh: T. & T. Clark, 1899.

Thomas, Robert L. *Understanding Spiritual Gifts: The Christian's Special Gifts in the Light of 1 Corinthians 12-14*. Chicago: Moody Press, 1978.

Tippett, Alan R. *Church Growth and the Word of God*. Grand Rapids: Wm. B. Eerdmans Publishing Company, 1970.

Towns, Elmer L. *Say-It-Faith*. Wheaton, Ill.: Tyndale House Publishers, 1983.

_____. *The Successful Sunday School and Teachers Guidebook*. Carol Stream, Ill.: Creation House, 1980.

_____. *The Ten Largest Sunday Schools*. Grand Rapids, Mich.: Baker Book House, 1969.

_____. *The World's Largest Sunday School*. Nashville: Thomas Nelson Incorporated, 1974.

Towns, Elmer L. and Falwell, Jerry. *Capturing a Town for Christ*. Old Tappan, N.J.: Fleming H. Revell Company, 1973.

_____. *Church Aflame*. Nashville: Impact Books, 1971.

Towns, Elmer L., Vaughn, John N., and Seifert, David J. *The Complete Book of Church Growth*. Wheaton, Ill.: Tyndale House Publishers, 1981.

Underwood, B.E. *The Gifts of the Spirit*. Franklin Springs, Ga.: Advocate Press, 1967.

Wagner, C. Peter. *Our Kind of People: The Ethical Dimensions of Church Growth in America*. Atlanta: John Knox Press, 1979.

_____. *What Are We Missing?* (formerly *Look Out! The Pentecostals Are Coming*) Carol Stream, Ill.: Creation House, 1973.

_____. *Your Church Can Be Healthy*. Nashville: Abingdon Press, 1979.

_____. *Your Church Can Grow: Seven Vital Signs of a Healthy Church*. Glendale, Cal.: Regal Books, 1976.

_____. *Your Spiritual Gifts Can Help Your Church Grow*. Glendale, Cal.: Regal Books, 1979.

Whyte, H.A. *Charismatic Gifts*. Monroeville, Penn.: Banner Publishing Company, 1972.

Williams, Rodman J. *The Gift of the Holy Spirit Today*. Plainsfield, N.J.: Logos International, 1980.

PERIODICALS
Towns, Elmer L. "The Seventy-five Largest Sunday Schools in America." *Christian Life* (August 1970):15.

OTHER SOURCES
Friesen, Harold. "A Model for a Church in Ministry by Employing Spiritual Gifts Resulting in Spiritual and Numerical Growth." D.Min. Thesis, Fuller Theological Seminary, 1979.

Murphy, Edward F. "The Gifts of the Spirit and the Mission of the Church." M.A., Fuller Theological Seminary, 1972.

Rosenberry, Floyd E. "St. Paul's Teaching Concerning Spiritual Gifts and the Relevancy for the Church Today." Th.M. Thesis, Fuller Theological Seminary, 1960.

Shepherd, Steven D. "Spiritual Gifts as a Force for the Revitalization of the San Fernando Church of Christ." D.Min., Fuller Theological Seminary, 1977.

Struikmans, Stephen P. "Developing a Strategy of Ministry for an Ex-urban Church Through Spiritual Gifts." D.Min., Fuller Theological Seminary, 1979.

Towns, Elmer L. *Say-It-Faith.* Seven cassette tapes. Wheaton, Ill.: Domain Communication Ltd., 1982. Tape 2: *The Pathologies of Faith.*

Watney, Paul B. "Ministry Gifts: God's Provision for Effective Missions." D.Min. Thesis, Fuller Theological Seminary, 1979.

Wells, John Arthur. "The Development of a Team Approach to the Spiritual Gifts of Ministry." D.Min. Thesis, Fuller Theological Seminary, 1980.

DATE DUE

JUN - 5 1987			
NOV 1 6 1988			
NOV 2 8 1990			
OCT 1 8 2000			
OCT 2 6 2000			